Introduction to Vedic Knowledge

first volume:

The Study of Vedic Scriptures Along History

by Parama Karuna Devi

Copyright © 2012 Parama Karuna Devi

All rights reserved.

ISBN-10: 1482500361
ISBN-13: 978-1482500363

published by Jagannatha Vallabha Research Center
PAVAN House, Siddha Mahavira patana,

Puri 752002 Orissa

Web presence:

http://www.jagannathavallabha.com

http://www.facebook.com/ParamaKarunaDevi

http://jagannathavallabhavedicresearch.wordpress.com/

The Perception of Vedic Culture in Western History

This publication originates from the need to present in a simple, clear, objective and exhaustive way, the basic information about the original Vedic knowledge, that in the course of the centuries has often been confused by colonialist propaganda, through the writings of indologists belonging to the euro-centric Christian academic system (that were bent on refuting and demolishing the vedic scriptures rather than presenting them in a positive way) and through the cultural superimposition suffered by sincere students who only had access to very indirect material, already carefully chosen and filtered by professors or commentators that were afflicted by negative prejudice.

It was pope Onorius IV (1286-1287) who inaugurated in the West the study of oriental languages and precisely Hebrew, Greek and Arabic. He had studied at the University of Paris before entering the diplomatic career at the service of pope Clement IV (1265-1268), who sent him to celebrate the crowning of Charles d'Anjou as King of Sicily. After becoming pope, Onorius introduced in the University of Paris the new curriculum (*Studia linguarum*) aimed at building the linguistic knowledge required to understand the original texts of the Old and New Testament and the Coranic texts, that were the theological, ethical and philosophical foundations of the scholars which in those times were not subject to the Church of Rome: Jews, orthodox Christians and Muslims.

The Ecumenic Council of Wien (1311-1312) recognized the importance of Onorius' strategy and encouraged the creation of suitable departments in all the other European universities, that were then under the complete control of the Church of Rome. In fact, all the universities started as *Scholae monasticae* approved by the papal bull *Studia generalia*, and were managed by the cathedrals or monasteries and aimed at training priests, government officers, lawyers and pyhysicians that would remain strictly loyal to the Church of Rome. All the students received the clerical tonsure and were only subjected to the ecclesiastic legal authority and not to the authority of the King or any other government agency.

The passage from *Schola monastica* to University (*universitas magistrorum et scholarium*, "universal community of teachers and scholars") was specifically characterized by the creation of teachers' guilds that acquired a certain organizational autonomy from the parishes on which they initially depended. The first of such universities was recognized in Bologna in 1088, followed by those of Paris in 1150, Oxford (1167), Valencia (1208), Cambridge (1209), Salamanca (1218), Montpellier (1220) and Padova (1222).

The official language of all universities was Latin, even if the students - coming from all parts of Europe - were divided into "*nationes*". At the University of Paris these were France, Normandie, Picardie and England-Germany, which also included the students from Scandinavia and eastern Europe.

After attending the preliminary courses (*trivium*: Latin grammar, rhetoric and dialectics, and *quadrivium*: arithmetics, geometry, music and astronomy) the students proceeded to further degrees of specialization, importance and glory consisting in the studies of arts, natural philosophy, medicine, canonic law and theology.

That period saw the resurfacing of some ancient texts that had somehow escaped the anti-pagan devastation conducted by Christians during the previous millennium. However, the only "approved" author allowed to be studied was Aristotle, and his writings were adapted to support the Christian theology, as we can see in the famous *Summa Theologica* by Thomas Aquinas. There were also strict limitations on Aristotle's books: his prohibited texts included physics and metaphysics.

The arabic texts studied in that period were on mathematics, geometry, medicine and the commentaries on the fragments of Aristotle; the most famous authors were Avicenna e Averroè.

Avicenna (Abū 'Alī al-Ḥusayn ibn 'Abd Allāh ibn Sīnā, 980-1037 CE), considered the father of modern medicine and "avicennan logic", perhaps the greatest representative of the so-called "golden age of Islam".

He wrote *The Book of Healing* and the *Canon of Medicine*, based on the teachings of *Sushruta samhita* and *Charaka samhita* as well as the writings of Hyppocrates and Galen. He also explored Indian mathematics and aristotelic and neoplatonic philosophy.

Averroè (Abū l-Walīd Muhammad ibn Ahmad Muhammad ibn Rushd, 1126-1198), *qadi* of Sevilla and Cordoba like his father and grandfather, became famous for his logical refutations in defense of the philosophical search, that he presented as compatible and non-contrary to theology. Specifically, he wrote many famous translations with commentaries to the texts of Aristotle, that had become completely forgotten in the West.

His most important work, *The Destruction of Destruction* (*Tahāfut al-tahāfut*, in Latin *Destructio destructionis*) is a refutation of *The Destruction of the Philosophers* (*Tahāfut al-falāsifa*, in Latin *Destructio philosophorum*), the aggressive text in which Al Ghazali presented freedom of thinking as offensive against Islamic theology. Averroè also composed a voluminous text focused on the analysis of the Islamic religious doctrines of his times and a treatise on *General Medicine*. Because of his defense of the intrinsic value of culture and free thinking, Averroè was pronounced as heretic, exiled and kept under strict control until his death: this sentence is considered the turning point closing the brief period of the "golden age" of Islamic domination.

Aristotle's works were translated from Greek into Latin also by the monks of Saint Michel, including Giacomo Veneto, starting from 1127. However, the study of Aristotle's philosophy was merely aimed at creating Church leaders that were adequately equipped with the knowledge required to protect it and bring about its triumph at global level. Among the laureates from the University of Paris there were many popes, such as Celestine II, Adrian IV, Innocentius III and Onorius IV.

In his attempts at becoming independent from the Church of Rome, Henry VIII of England too established chairs of "Regius Professor" to teach Hebrew at Cambridge in 1540 and at Oxford in 1546; then a department of Arabic was established in Cambridge in 1643. In 1669 Edmund Castell published his "Dictionary of seven language", the *Lexicon Heptaglotton Hebraicum, Chaldaicum, Syriacum, Samaritanum, Aethiopicum, Arabicum, et Persicum*.

Of course, all the knowledge offered in the universities had to be subordinated to the Christian doctrine: only in the 19th century, after the French revolution and Napoleon's regime, theology ceased to be a compulsory study in the universities - first in Paris and then in Oxford.

Indology proper (as the study of Sanskrit and Vedic texts) only started after a new sea route to the Indies became feasible. During the period of Islamic expansion, commerce with India was strictly controlled and exploited by Muslims, therefore the European kingdoms suffered great economic losses due to the extreme rise in the cost of spices. At that time, spices were used as medicines, flavorings and preservatives for food, as well as ingredients for perfumes and scents for body, clothing and houses. We need to remember that in that period there was no refrigeration system, the Christian rules discouraged people from taking baths and toilets were seriously rudimentary.

The crusades failed in their attempt to take the Middle East away from Islam, and south Europe had to engage in a hard war on its very territory - Spain, south Italy, Greece - to fight back the invasions of the "Sarrasins". Only in 1491 the King of Spain was able to retake Grenada from the hands of the Muslims. When Constantinople fell in the hands of the Turks, the European monarchs started to seek urgently for a sea route that could allow them to reach the Indies without having to travel through the territories occupied by Islam. This was precisely the plan of Christopher Columbus, as when he started his journey in 1492 he was not looking for America but rather for India, It was also the plan of Vasco da Gama (journey from 1497 to 1499), Magellan (journey of 1519-1522) and other great navigators of those times. The explicit ambition of those monarchs was the direct conquest of the territories and their resources, to be exploited for the greater power of Christianity, so each expedition was accompanied by an ambassador of the Church of Rome, who was to report everything to the pope.

Francis (Francisco) Xavier de Jasso y Azpilicueta (1506-1552) had graduated from Paris University together with Ignatius Loyola and Pierre Favre. He left in 1549 to accompany the Portuguese expedition of Vasco da Gama and organize India's christianization. Initially Xavier had founded the Jesuit order together with Ignatius of Loyola and other 5 friends, with the declared purpose of "converting all the Muslims of the Middle East", but as that task had proven impossible, the Company of Jesus shifted its attention to the fabulous Indies.

The Portuguese expedition landed at Goa, on the west coast of India, taking possession of the territory in the name of the pope and immediately founding the College of Saint Paul, a seminar to train lay priests, that was entrusted to by Michele Ruggieri. This became the headquarters of the Jesuits in Asia, the base from which Nobili, Ricci and Beschi started for their missions respectively to India and to the Far East.

In India, Roberto de Nobili (1577-1656) developed the method of inculturation (*accommodatio*), that had already been successfully applied in Europe in the early centuries of Christianity (for example with the Christmas tree, Easter eggs, the processions of the saints, etc) adopting and adapting those Indian traditions and customs that could make Christianity "more digestible" for the natives. He dressed as a *sannyasi*, with a shaved head and *sikha*, and utilized terms in Sanskrit and Tamil - for example calling "Veda" the Bible and "Guru" the Christian priest. He also explained the *brahmanas'* sacred thread as a symbol of Christian Trinity and so on.

All over the occupied region Xavier destroyed the temples, the sacred places and the religious scriptures, that he openly denounced as "works of the devil, repellent and grotesque", applying the usual brutal ways to force the native population to convert to Christianity.

All the *brahmanas* were killed or expelled together with their books, and the population was forced to regularly gather in churches to listen to the preaching against their own religion. All the texts that were not written in Portuguese language were burned, no matter what their subject was.

Xavier was particularly interested in children and he removed them from their families "to educate them in a Christian way". Still today in India we find innumerable schools and especially institutes of higher studies - colleges and universities - dedicated to the name of Francis Xavier, and still today it is normal among Hindus to call "idols" the sacred images of their own religion and "mythology" the sacred stories contained in *Upanishads*, *Puranas* and *Itihasas* - so much that people have difficulties in understanding why such definitions are incorrect and inadequate to refer to the objects of their own faith.

In his diaries, Xavier wrote about the children educated by the Jesuits: "Their hatred for idolatry is wonderful. They revolt against the heathens and when they see their own parents engaging in pagan practices, they scold them and come at once to me to report. As soon as I know about one such situation, I go to the spot with a band of these children, who immediately shower the devil with an amount of insult and damage greater than what was the amount of honor and worship it had received from parents, relatives and friends. The children jump on the idols, they throw them down, break them to pieces, spit on them, trample them under their feet and kick them around - in short, they do them all possible offense. I order to destroy the huts where the idols were kept, and to shatter the idols into the smallest pieces possible. I would never end to describe the great consolation that fills my soul when I see this destruction of the idols by the hands of the idolaters themselves. I cannot describe the happiness I feel watching the idols cast down and destroyed by those same people that once used to worship them. If in spite of all good advice someone persists in making idols, we have him punished by the chief of the village, who sentences him to exile, and we burn his house as a warning for the others."

Besides tirelessly carrying on with this kind of preaching, Xavier repeatedly asked both the pope and the King of Portugal to introduce the Inquisition in India (where it continued in full swing until 1812) to uproot all traces of paganism as well as heresy and even punish scarce enthusiasm in the Christian faith. The local Penal Code of the Inquisition filled 320 pages with the list of prohibitions, and the punishments for the rebels were considered by all contemporaries as the heaviest ever applied by the Portuguese catholic Church. Still today the region of Goa is strongly Catholic, and the remnants of Francis Xavier's body are worshiped as a relic in the main basilica.

The two great maritime and colonial powers in those times were Portugal and Spain, to which pope Martin V assigned the entire world as legal possession with the bulla *Rex Regnum*, giving them "right of crusade and conquest" on all the territories they would find, each on either side of the famous "Tordesillas line" that divided the planet into two halves. The Portugal was given Africa and Asia, while Spain was assigned the new territories of the Americas.

The kingdoms of Britain, France and Holland, that were politically non-aligned with the pope and therefore "not authorized" to conquer lands outside Europe, organized first their pirate fleets to grab whatever they could of the immense wealth transported home by the Spanish and Portuguese fleets. Soon they realized that it was much easier and convenient to establish their own colonies in the New World dealing directly with the natives, who did not seem to care much for the authority of the pope in Rome or Christianity in general.

After the battle of Gravelines (1588) and the famous defeat of the Spanish Invincible Armada that was trying to invade the English coasts, and the two subsequent Spanish failures of 1596 and 1597, England became the greatest maritime and colonial power of the times, under the enlightened reign of Elizabeth I. Already in 1600 the Queen created the East India Trading Company with the status of English Royal Charter. The Company practically had the European monopoly of trade on tea, cotton, silk, indigo and opium, with a strong competitor in the Dutch equivalent of East India Trading Company, that was dealing mostly with spices, cocoa, coffee, sugar etc.

In the subsequent centuries England founded colonies of migrants in north America and Australia, and established a strong commercial and political control on India. In 1670 king Charles II gave the Company the right to acquire territories independently, to mint currency, hold forts and command army troops, establish alliances, wage war and sign peace treaties, exercing full civil and criminal jurisdiction on the territories it acquired. The British regime in India had started.

William Carey (1761-1834), founder of the Baptist Missionary Society, published in 1792 the volume *An Enquiry into the Obligations of Christians to use means for the Conversion of the Heathens*. To further his mission, he started to study oriental languages and with the help of one Pandit Mrityunjay he compiled a series of dictionaries of the local languages. From his Serampore Mission press, near Calcutta, he printed over 200 thousands Bibles in 45 Indian and oriental languages (including Oriya, Hindi, Tamil, Sikh, Parsi, Sindhi, Nepali, Armenian, Afghan, Gujarati, Bhutani, Javanese, Siamese and Sinhalese) and started to train a group of "Christian pundits" who studied the Vedic scriptures to refute and oppose them. He also started the publication of school texts for the Fort William

College and for the Calcutta School Book Society, as well as the first monthly magazine and then the first daily newspaper in Bengali, starting from 1818. His organization also produced the paper for the printing.

Charles Grant (1746-1823), president of the East India Company, was an ardent activist of the Evangelic party led by William Wilberforce (1759-1833). Under his protection Claudius Bucchanan arrived in 1790 at Calcutta; Bucchanan was convinced that God had delivered India into the hands of the British for the only purpose of christianizing the Hindus, liberating them from "the yoke of the dark and degrading, monstrous and absurd superstitions of their native faith." After becoming vice president of the Serampore College, Bucchanan journeyed to Orissa in 1805 briging back deeply distorted descriptions of the "Moloch Jaggernauth" to whom - according to him - thousands of human sacrifices were offered during the annual Ratha yatra at Puri, the "Mecca or Jerusalem of the Hindoos, the Sebastopol of their idolatry".

In 1797 Charles Grant wrote a libel entitled *Observations on the State among the Asiatic Subjects of Great Britain, particularly with respect to morals and means of improving them*, in which he clearly expressed his intention to introduce to India a strictly Christian school system aimed at demolishing Vedic culture. His Evangelist fellow A.H. Bowman wrote, "Hinduism is a great philosophy which lives on unchanged whilst other systems are dead, which as yet un supplanted has its stronghold in Vedanta, the last and the most subtle and powerful foe of Christianity." This hostile approach was obviously inspired and supported by the university academics, still heavily under the control of Christianity - specifically, in Britan it was Anglican Protestantism, in which the monarch (now emperor of the colonies) was the highest religious authority.

Horace Hayman Wilson (1786-1860), graduated in Medicine at the St Thomas Hospital, arrived in India as assistant surgeon with the East India Company and became secretary (from 1811 to 1833) and then director (from 1837 to 1860) of the Royal Asiatic Society of Bengal. He translated the *Meghaduta* by Kalidasa and the *Vishnu Purana*, then in 1819 he published the first English-Sanskrit dictionary and helped Mill to compile his famous historical treatise. He was the first to obtain the post of Professor for the Boden Chair of Sanskrit at Oxford in 1833 and he immediately announced a prize of 200 sterling pounds for "the best refutation of the Hindu religious system".

After him, the Boden Chair went to Sir Monier-Williams (1819-1899, author of the most famous and still popularly used Sanskrit/English dictionary), who wrote, "For what purpose then has this enormous territory been committed to England? Not to be the 'corpus vile' of political, social, or military experiments; not for benefit of our commerce, or the increase of our wealth - but that every man, woman and child, from Cape Comorin to the Himalaya mountains, may be elevated, enlightened Christianized... When the walls of the mighty fortress of

Brahmanism are encircled, undermined, and finally stormed by the solders of the cross, the victory of Christianity must be signal and complete."

Contrarily to what had been done by the Portuguese government in Goa, where the catholic Inquisition had been imposed by force, the British colonial government strictly maintained a neutral facade, that was necessary in order to avoid the indignation and the violent rebellion of 50 million Indians against the 30 thousand Britishers staying in India. The documents of that period show that sometimes this motivation was also openly declared, as for example by Mr. Twinning, pioneer of the tea trade, and by Colonel Montgomery, commander in chief of the British army in India. Under the governatorate of Lord Cornwallis (1786-1805) the official position of the colonial government was to "preserve the laws of the Shaster and the Koran, and to protect the natives of India in the free exercise of their religion," but the missionaries were not only tolerated but even actively helped, because this was convenient for the colonial purposes. The British prime minister, Lord Palmerston (Henry John Temple, 3rd viscount of Palmerston, in office from 1807 until his death in 1865) declared, "It is not only our duty, but in our own interest to promote the diffusion of Christianity as far as possible throughout the length and breadth of India".

Secretary of State Lord Halifax (1881-1959), too, was of the same opinion: " Every additional Christian is an additional bond of union with this country and an additional source of strength to the Empire."

It is interesting to notice that Lord Halifax, also known as Edward Frederick Lindley Wood, first Earl of Halifax, remained in charge as Secretary for Foreign Affairs from 1938 to 1940, and was appointed Viceroy of India from 1926 to 1931 with the additional title of Baron of Irwin on direct recommendation of King George V, also because Edward's grandfather had been Secretary of State for India. In that position, and under the direct pressure of the British King, Lord Halifax took a series of disastrous decisions with the aim of severely repressing the Indian independence movement.

Thomas Babbington Macaulay (1800-1859), first Legislator Lord under the General Governor of India, was given the task to organize the academic system in India precisely in this direction. In a 1836 letter to his father, Macaulay wrote, "It is my belief that if our plans of education are followed up, there will not be a single idolator among the respectable classes in Bengal thirty years hence... No Hindu who has received an English education ever remains sincerely attached to his religion."

The missionary Alexander Duff (1806-1878) founded in Calcutta the famous Scottish Churches College, which he envisioned as a "headquarters for a great campaign against Hinduism." He trained students from the wealthy classes of Indian society and possibly from the "high castes" to learn the language and ideals of the colonial government, thus shaping the impressionable minds of the youngsters into the firm belief in the superiority of Christianity and European civilization, for the purpose of creating an intermediate class of "brown sahibs" that would control the native masses for them. The cultural battle against Hinduism was well beyond the scope of the British colonial government: the christianization of the entire world was presented as "the white man's burden" - the duty and mission of each European.

Amongs the many others, Baron von Bunsen, ambassador of Prussia in England, dreamed about converting the entire world to Christianity. His protegé Fredrich Max Mueller (1823-1900), born in Dessau (Germany), studied Sanskrit at Leipzig and translated the *Hitopadesa* before arriving in England in 1846. He was introduced to Macauley and obtained from the East India Company the task to translate the *Rig Veda* into English - 4 shillings a page. After settling in Oxford, Max Mueller translated many other texts and wrote the encyclopedia *The Sacred Books of the East* (50 volumes, started in 1875). He wrote, "This edition of mine and the translation of the Veda will hereafter tell to a great extent... the fate of India, and on the growth of millions of souls in that country.... the only way of uprooting all that has sprung from it during the last 3000 years... and that is of a more degraded and savage character than the worship of Jupiter, Apollo or Minerva... It may have but served to prepare the way of Christ... India is much riper for Christianity than Rome or Greece were at the time of Saint Paul."

Max Muller was particularly irked by those scholars who, instead of devoting themselves to this "evangelic mission", committed the mortal sin to sincerely appreciate Vedic knowledge: one who did that "should know that he can expect no money; nay, he should himself wish for no mercy, but invite the heaviest artillery... to condone Brahminical idolatry and to discountenance Christianity is to commit high treason against humanity and civilization."

One of such rebels was Louis Jacolliot (1837-1890), a French scholar that for a period became supreme Judge in the court of Chandranagar for the colonial regime. In his book *The Bible in India*, Jacolliot wrote, "O Land of ancient India! O Cradle of Humanity, hail! Hail revered motherland whom centuries of brutal invasions have not yet buried under the dust of oblivion. Hail, Fatherland of faith, of love, of poetry and of science. May we hail a revival of thy past in our Western future... How glorious the epoch that then presented itself to my study and comprehension! ... I enquired of monuments and ruins, I questioned the Vedas whose pages count their existence by thousands of years and whence enquiring youth imbibed the science of life long before Thebes of the hundred gates or Babylon the great had traced their foundations.... And then India appears to me in all the living power of her originality – I traced her progress in the expansion of her enlightenment over the world – I saw her giving her laws, her customs, her morale, her religion to Egypt, to Persia, to Greece and Rome... Name of us any modern discovery, and we venture to say that Indian history need not long be searched before the prototype will be found on record... we may read what Manu said, perhaps 10,000 years before the birth of Christ: The first germ of life was developed by water and heat. Water ascends towards the sky in vapors; from the sun it descends in rain, from the rains are born the plants, and from the plants, animals. ... India of the Vedas entertained a respect for women amounting to worship; a fact which we seem little to suspect in Europe when we accuse the extreme East of having denied the dignity of woman, and of having only made her an instrument of pleasure and of passive obedience."

Even the officers of the British government were often very impressed by Vedic culture. In 1689, John Ovington (the King's chaplain) wrote *A Voyage to Surat*, where he said, "Of all the regions of the Earth (India is) the only Public theatre of Justice and Tenderness to Brutes and all living creatures." He also found that, because of their (vegetarian) diet, the Hindus kept "a comely and proportionate body and lived a long life. The simple and meatless food made their thoughts quick and nimble, their comprehension of things easier and developed in them a spirit of fearlessness."

In 1690 the diplomat Sir William Temple wrote in his *Essay upon the Ancient and Modern Learning*, "it seems most probable that Pythagoras learned, and transported into Greece and Italy, the greatest part of his natural and moral philosophy, rather than from the Aegyptians... Nor does it seem unlikely that the Aegyptians themselves might have drawn much of their learning from the Indians long before."

Lord Warren Hastings (1732-1818), first governor general of India (from 1773 to 1785), wrote, "The writers of the Indian philosophies will survive, when the British dominion in India shall long have ceased to exist, and when the sources which it yielded of wealth and power are lost to remembrances."

Sir Thomas Munro (1761-1827), officer of the British government and governor of Madras (in 1819) stated to the House of Commons, "If a good system of agriculture, unrivalled manufacturing skill, a capacity to produce whatever can contribute to convenience or luxury, schools established in every village for teaching, reading, writing and arithmetic; the general practice of hospitality and charity among each other; and above all, a treatment of the female sex full of confidence, respect, and delicacy, (if all these) are among the signs which denote a civilized people, then the Hindus, are not inferior to the nations of Europe; and if civilization is to become an article of trade between England and India, I am convinced that England will gain by the import cargo."

Colonel James Tod (1782-1835) wrote in his *Annals and Antiquities of Rajasthan: or the Central and Western Rajput States of India*: "sages like those whose systems of philosophy were prototypes of those of Greece: to whose works Plato, Thales & Pythagoras were disciples? Where do I find astronomers whose knowledge of planetary systems yet excites wonder in Europe as well as the architects and sculptors whose works claim our admiration, and the musicians who could make the mind oscillate from joy to sorrow, from tears to smile..."

In 1887 Sir William Wedderburn Bart (1838 - 1918), magistrate in Pune and chief secretary to the government in Bombay, wrote, "The Indian village has thus for centuries remained a bulwark against political disorder, and the home of the simple domestic and social virtues."

Sir John Malcolm (1829-1896), governor of Bombay, wrote, "The Hindoo...are distinguished for some of the finest qualities of the mind; they are brave, generous, and humane, and their truth is as remarkable as their courage."

Lord Curzon (1859-1925), Marquis of Kedleston, was viceroy of India from 1899 to 1905. In a speech in Delhi in 1901 he said, "Powerful Empires existed and flourished here [in India] while Englishmen were still wandering painted in the woods."

Sir Charles Norton Edgcumbe Eliot (1864-1931) similarly stated, "Let me confess that I cannot share the confidence in the superiority of Europeans and their ways which is prevalent in the West... Hinduism has not been made, but has grown. It is a jungle, not a building. It is a living example of a great national paganism such as might have existed in Europe if Christianity had not become the state religion of the Roman Empire."

He also liked to quote the *Taittirya Upanishad* (3.6): "Bliss is Brahman, for from bliss all these being are born, by bliss when born they live, into bliss they enter at their death."

Even Francis Yeats-Brown (1886-1944), officer of the Bengal Lancers, was attracted to the study of Vedic knowledge and yoga, and ended up writing a book on these topics (*Yoga Explained*).

However, the British officer to be most impressively transformed by the Indian experience was Sir John Woodroffe, also known as Arthur Avalon (1865-1936), general advocate for Bengal during a period of 18 years and supreme magistrate in 1915. The study of Sanskrit and vedic scriptures conquered him to the point he personally adopted the traditional Indian clothing (*dhoti*). His greatest interest was for Yoga and Tantra, which he considered the greatest expression of India's religious spirit, with is deep symbolism and secret philosophical aspects. He translated many original texts and published several treatises including the famous *The Serpent Power*, and gave innumerable lectures and presentations. He wrote, "I believe that the East and particularly India possesses that which is the highest value. I wish to see this preserved for the mutual benefit of East and West... An examination of the Vedic thesis shows that it is in conformity with the most advanced philosophical and scientific thoughts of the West and, where this is not so, it is the scientist who will go to the Vedantist and not the Vedantist to the scientist... In India there has been intellectual and spiritual freedom - the most valuable of all... As the Veda says, Truth will conquer."

Sir William Jones (1746-1794), graduated from Oxford, was appointed judge of the supreme court in Calcutta; during his stay in India he started to study Sanskrit and founded the Royal Asiatic Society of Bengal. He was fluent in 13 languages and knew 28 more rather well, and probably this is why he was the first to see a relationship between Sanskrit, Greek and Latin, and more distantly with Goth and the other Celtic languages, and with ancient Persian. Starting from these observations, he formulated the famous theory of an ancient indo-european civilization, and the belief that Pythagoras and Plato had tapped the Indian wisdom of Vedanta to develop their philosophical systems. He wrote poems dedicated to Narayana, Lakshmi and Ganga, and he declared himself to be in love with the *gopis*, charmed with Krishna, an enthusiastic admirer of Rama and a devout adorer of Brihma (Brahma), Bishen (Vishnu), Mahisher (Maheshwara)".

He encouraged his colleague Charles Wilkins to produce the first English translation of *Bhagavad gita* and inspired many other later men of culture, such as Schopenhauer (who mentioned him in various writings) and indirectly the poets of the romantic movement, such as Lord Byron and Samuel Taylor Coleridge. Jones was heavily criticized by James Mill (father of the philosopher John Stuart Mill), that in 1818 had written for the government the voluminous *History of British India* greatly based on the description of the notorious French missionary Abbé Dubois. Mill's treatise was one of the compulsory texts at the Haileybury College, training the government officers that were going to serve in India.

Many scholars have noticed a strong connection of the ancient Vedic knowledge with Greek culture, still considered by mainstream academia as the origin of western culture. It is well known that in ancient times culture freely circulated in the form of books, teachers, religious people and scholars, traveling along the rich commercial routes both by sea and by land. Merchants of all nations used to establish small colonies in the countries where they had commercial interests, and often facilitated the traveling and settlement of fellow countrymen who wanted to emigrate for various reasons. Both the caravans and the cargo ships were happy to accept passengers traveling in both directions, connecting India with the mediterranean and middle-eastern countries such as Greece, Rome, Egypt, Phoenicia, Anatolia and Mesopotamia. This is how culture spread - philosophy, religion and sciences, that in the ancient world were considered all harmonious parts of the One Knowledge.

The first "foreign" scholars to approach Vedic knowledge were probably the Greek philosophers, who even before the advent of Alexander the Great went to study in the famous universities of Nalanda and Takshila, that were nearest to the western boundaries of India. Indians, too, traveled often, and there is evidence of the presence of *brahmanas* and Buddhist monks in Greece, especially in Athens, even before Socrates.

Eusebius and Aristoxenes speak about them, and there is also a fragment of Aristotle's preserved in the writings of Diogenes Laertius, specifically in his *Biography of Pythagoras*.

Another of Pythagoras' biographers, Iamblichus (582-506 BCE), clearly states that the great philosopher and mathematician visited India during his study journeys. Certainly during his traveling he had the opportunity to study the *Sulba sutras*, the section of Vedic scriptures that deals with mathematics, containing the theorem that is known today as "Pythagoras' theorem" (the quadrature of the hypotenuse), as well as the square root of 2 correct to the fifth decimal, and other jewels of knowledge. The oldest existing copy of the *Sulba sutra* is a transcription by Baudhayana, traced back at least to the 8th century BCE.

Among the Vedic concepts embraced by Greek scholars there are certainly mathematics and geometry, music, cosmology, astronomy, physics, medicine, metallurgy as well as metaphysics or philosophy, religious symbolism and the awareness of the unity of life. Specifically, the compassionate awareness of the common nature of all beings gave rise to ethical vegetarianism, of which the pythagoreans became the main exponents, so much that until the 20th century in Europe all vegetarians were called pythagoreans.

In *Phedo*, Plato describes silent meditation as the withdrawing of the senses from their objects and stopping the flow of the movements of the mind. To understand how deeply ancient Greeks absorbed the religion of Vedic India it is sufficient to compare the image of the Omphalos ("the navel of the world"), center of the Orphic cult at Delphi and in the entire Mediterranean region, with the picture of any Shiva linga.

Another great personality that certainly visited India was Apollonius Tyanaeus, neopythagorean philosopher hailing from Cappadocia, compared by the christians of the 4th century to Jesus himself. Apollonius' biographer Philostratus speaks of his journey to India in 2 chapters of the book he wrote in 210 CE. He also writes, "Everyone wishes to live near God, but only Hindus succeed in doing that."

A contemporary of Philostratus, Lucius Flavius Arrianus also known as Xenophon (86 - 160 CE) compiled the *Anabasis Alexandri*, the story of the campaigns of Alexander the Great, based on the writing of Ptolemy (the most important general in Alexander's army), Callisthenes (the nephew of Aristotle, Alexander's tutor), Onesicritus, Nearchus and Aristobulus, all contemporaries of Alexander. Here is how Xenophon describes the Indians: "They are remarkably brave, and the best warriors among all the Asians. They give enormous value to moral integrity and truthfulness, they are so honest that they do not use bolts for their doors or written contracts for their agreements. They are so reasonable that rarely they require the intervention of judges to regulate their disagreements... It is also remarkable how in India all Indians are free and there is no slavery. Their armies have never invaded foreign countries with the purpose of conquest."

Many peoples came in contact with Vedic culture and were fascinated by it to the point that they spontaneoulsy chose to embrace it, and yet they remained completely independent politically; the *Mahabharata* lists several of them among the allies of the Pandavas or the Kurus that took part in the Kurukshetra war.

After his brief and unsuccessful campaign in India, Alexander the Great returned to the West with a great quantity of Vedic texts and a numerous group of translators and copiers, that settled in the new capital called Alexandria of Egypt and became the foundation of the very famous library and university of Alexandria, where many hundreds of thousands of texts were preserved.

Hellenistic culture was perfectly compatible with vedic knowledge and religion, yet there were also some who chose to fully embrace the Hindu orthodox tradition, especially Vaishnavism.

In India we still find the famous column of Heliodorus the son of Dion, Greek ambassador for the King Antiakila of Bactria, who was envoyed to the court of King Bhagabhadra of Varanasi in the 2nd century BCE.

This Heliodorus was so taken with Indian spirituality that he officially converted to Hinduism, becoming a devotee of Vishnu, and erected a commemorative pillar with a

Sanskrit (Brahmi) inscription to praise "Vasudeva, the God of all Gods, who rides Garuda".

Still in 662 CE, Severus Sebokht di Nisibis, christian bishop of Kenneserin in Syria, although condemning astrologers of all denominations, was very favorably impressed by the "knowledge of the Hindus, their subtle and ingenuous discoveries, superior to those of the Greeks and Babylonians, of their rational mathematical system and calculation method (the decimal system) that no words can praise enough".

Trade and cultural exchanges continued for many centuries also between the western ports of India and Egypt - one example for all, the five ships sent by Queen Hatsheput to purchase spices - and between India and the ancient kingdom of Israel at the times of Solomon. These contacts continued with the Alexandria of the Ptolemies and with Rome. At Muziris (now Cranganore, in Kerala) there was a garrison of 1200 legionaries guarding the Roman merchants' colony. In the same period some colonies of Jewish traders settled in the area.

The ports of the east coast of India were the base of trading and cultural exchanges with the countries of the far east. The greatest Chinese river, the Yang-tze, received its name in honor of the Ganges. Hu Shih, ambassador of China in the United States, declared, "India conquered and dominated culturally China for 20 centuries, without ever sending one single soldier beyond the borders."

Ancient Indians founded many colonies (collectively called Svarnabhumi) all around Indonesia up to Singapore (originally called Sinha Puri, "the city of the lion"). Still today we can see in Cambodia one of the largest Hindu temples in the religious complex of Angkor Vat, and of course we must remember the huge spreading of Buddhism in the far east - Buddhism being derived without interruptions from Vedic culture and still sharing many ideas with it.

After the fall of the Roman empire and with the advent of Islam, it was the Muslims that controlled access to India. They, too, studied the scientific discoveries of the Vedic civilization and percolated some of them into the regions of Europe they had conquered.

Already in 638 Khalifa Umar launched a campaign to conquer India, particularly the region that is today known as Beluchistan. From 638 to 715 these invasions were regularly contained and pushed back by the Baluch princes of Makaran. The Arab chronicles of the time attribute such defeats to the "black magic" apparently used in the mysterious weapons of the Hindus - who became famous as the great magicians of the Arabian tales, developing into legends such as those of the *Arabian Nights*.

Since the ethical code of the *kshatriyas* did not allow the persecution of defeated enemies, the Hindu princes stopped fighting as soon as their opponents accepted defeat, and when the enemies surrendered they were allowed to enter freely into the territories and approach the population without restrictions, as long as they abstained from any form of violence. Actually all visitors and foreigners were offered great honors, as enjoined by the vedic teaching *atithi devo bhava*, "a guest must be respected like God himself".

This gave the Arab invaders the opportunity to come in contact with the texts and the teachers of Vedic knowledge. The fourth Khalifa Ali bin Abi Talib (656-661 CE) described India as "the land where books were written for the first time, and where wisdom and knowledge were born". In the 9th century the historian Yaqubi wrote, "Hindus are superior to all other nations for intelligence and thoughtfulness. They are the most precise in astronomy and astrology, and the most expert in medicine. Greeks and Persians have gained much from their knowledge." Another Muslim historian of the 9th century, Al Jahiz, commented, "the Hindus excel in mathematics and in the other sciences, they have perfected the arts such as sculpture, painting and architecture, and have collections of poetry, philosophy, literature and ethical sciences. They are wise, brave, and possess the virtues of cleanliness and purity".

After consolidating their knowledge of Indian society and its territory, and fearing the growing Hindu religious and cultural influence on their own lands (especially on the sufi movement), the Arabs returned to their aggression plans and in 711 Mohammed-ibn-Qasim took possession of Deval (presently Debal, near Karachi) by blackmailing the guardian of the fortress gates. He kidnapped his 3 children, beheaded one of them and threatened he would kill the other two if the gate keeper refused to open for him a secondary secret door that led into the walls.

Once the Sindh was occupied, the invaders focused on Rajasthan and Gujarat, attacking respectively the Rajputana and Chalukya (Solanki) princes, who successfully defended their territories. In 980 there was a second wave of invasions by the "new Muslims" of the islamized regions of Persia, Turkey and Mongolia. The army of the Persian Sabuktgin occupied Kubha (now Kabul, in Afghanistan) by exploiting the Hindu princes' ethical code in war, according to which one should not attack an enemy who is not ready for battle. So the Sultan dressed his soldiers in black, wrapped the horses' hooves with cloth to muffle the sound of their steps, and attacked the Hindu army camp in the middle of the night, when all the warriors had gone peacefully to sleep. In the confusion and surprise, almost all the warriors were killed before they had the time to get their weapons. The few survivors, including prince Anandapala the son of King Jayapala, withdrew to Ubandapura (presently Und in Pakistan) in the kingdom of Pakhtunisthan. That region, too, was invaded by the muslims, who won the Lahore battle by secretly administering a slow effect poison to the war elephants in the Hindu army.

The 17 years old Trilochanapala, son of Anantapala, was crowned king and moved the capital to Kangra (Himachal Pradesh); in 1020 he was killed by a small group of Muslims disguised as Hindu *sannyasis*, who insisted to meet him in his apartment to deliver a secret message. The fake *sadhus* cut the prince's throat and left the decapitated body with a message stating that "all those who opposed Allah's soldiers would suffer the same fate". The subsequent attack to the Kangra fort found the defenders still shocked, confused and without a leader, so almost all the inhabitants fled to the mountains.

The way to the subcontinent was opened: the Persian Sultan Mahmud Ghazni, son of Sabuktgin, immediately started a series of regular incursions against Purushapura (Peshawar), Lavakushpura (Lahore), Mulasthana (Multan), Somanath, Palitana, Staneshvara (Thanesar), Mathura, Kannauj and Khajuraho, looting treasures and enslaving the local people, that were sent through the Himalayan passes of the Hindu Kush ("the Hindu killer"), a territory that earned that name because the Hindu slaves were forced to carry the looted treasures by walking to the inner lands of their conquerors, and at every journey they died in their thousands of exhaustion, cold and starvation.

From 1033 to 1187 the islamic power in India became consolidated, and the Sultans investigated more deeply into Indian culture. With the new Sultan Mohammed Ghori, belonging to the second generation of Indian converts (the Gauris had been cowherd men subject to the Solanki princes) the situation changed drastically. Now the invaders had no more need to collect information from the local Hindus, therefore all masks were thrown aside. In 1191 Ghori attacked Prithviraj

Chauhan, Maharaja Rajput of Shaka Ambara, but he was defeated; Ghori's army escaped by covering their retreat with a herd of cows chained to one another, so that the Hindu warriors could not advance without killing the innocent animals.

After being defeated, Ghori proposed the peace, begging forgiveness for his aggression and calling the Maharaja "brother"; he was allowed to go free and the Maharaja even gave him an escort with 500 horses and 20 elephants. But as soon as he was out of reach, Ghori massacred his escort and sent their heads to the Maharaja, then immediately resumed his attacks. Finally he defeated the Hindu King by challenging him to a personal duel, and instead capturing him as a prisoner. The Maharaja was chained, force-fed opium and paraded in that condition in front of the Rajput army, then his eyes were carved out and he was kept as a slave in the court of Ghori. The entire territory conquered by Ghori was then submitted to the strict islamic law: all the Vedic texts were destroyed, the *brahmanas* slaughtered or forced to convert, the temples razed to the ground (and mosques were built in their place) and the Persian language was imposed as the only allowed language (which later became the present Urdu-Hindu). The "infidels" could continue to practice their religion but only in a strictly private way, and only by submitting to a constant system of limitations and humiliations. All the non-Muslims were given a legal status of permanent slavery (*zimma*), under the power of a local Muslim owner (*zamindar*) to whom they had to pay a "survival tax" just to avoid being killed, plus the rent for the land they lived on (*kharaj*), and various other and completely new taxes. Only a Muslim could ride (horses etc) or carry weapons. The non-Muslims had no right to disobey any order given them by a Muslim, build a house that was taller than the house of the poorest Muslim in the region, build new temples or repair the old or damaged temples, teach or study texts that were "contrary to Islam". Non-Muslims also had to submit to a series of rules for clothing (for example the prohibition to wear shoes) and restrictions in social life and professional occupation, specifically engineered to make life extremely difficult to those who chose not to convert to Islam.

The islamic invasion also wiped out Buddhism - an essentially monastic, non-violent and non-political system that until then had survived and thrived under the protection of the Hindu princes. The Muslims saw the Buddhists as even more "infidel" than Hindus, because Buddhism denies the existence of God and the soul. The monks that survived the destruction of the Buddhist university centers escaped to Tibet, Lanka and the regions east of India, where they started to thrive again under the local monarchs.

In 1192 the islamic invaders took Hastinapura (Delhi); from there they swarmed into the Ganges plain down to present Bangladesh, imposing the fundamentalist islamic government in the regions they were occupying. The Bengal sultanate became the easter counterpart of the sultanate of Delhi, with which it often clashed for the supremacy on the subcontinent. In 1326 the Muslims arrived in south India, seizing a large part of the territory; the city of Madras took its name from the *madrassa* (islamic religious school) that made it famous, and the name of Hyderabad, in central-south India, was imposed to the pre-existing city. The same thing happened with Allahabad (ancient Prayaga), Ahmedabad and many other cities.

For some time the hindu kingdom of Vijayanagara resisted in the region, fighting successfully from 1331 to 1565 against the Bahamani sultans that had settled in present Andhra pradesh. At that time Vijayanagara became the only shelter for the *brahmanas* and the teachers of Vedic knowledge, until 1565 when this last Hindu stronghold was stormed, his inhabitants slaughtered to the last, and all buildings totally destroyed during 6 continuous months of looting and destruction.

The islamic control on the Indian subcontinent was opposed in Maharashtra by Maharatha Chatrapati Shivaji, and in Kashmir and Punjab by Sikhism, originally founded by Guru Nanak and transformed into the combative Khalsa Panth by Guru Tegh Bahadur and Guru Gobind Singh.

The Marathas fought the Mughals from 1674 to 1701, when they succeeded in reclaiming a great part of the subcontinent to hindu rule; however from 1775 the Marathas were engaged in wars by the British and were finally defeated in 1818. Similarly, the Sikh empire developed in the north (Panjab, Kashmir, Sindh etc) from 1799 to 1849, when it was dissolved by the British. The Kings of Orissa also defended their territories from 1212 (the time of the first invasion) to 1567, when the Afghans declared their independence from the Moghul empire and established themselves in Orissa, to be briefly substituted by the Marathas and then by the British.

However, by and large over several centuries the islamic fundamentalists were able to conduct their systematic persecutions against the tradition of Vedic knowledge. One important exception was Muhammad Dara Shikoh (1627-1658), son of the Moghul emperor Shah Jahan. The *mullahs* did not like Muhammad Dara because of his sufi heterodoxy and his admiration for Vedic knowledge; he was particularly fascinated by the *Upanishads* and translated 50 of them under the title of *Sirr i Akbar* ("the Great Secret"), a book that also included quotes from *Bhagavad gita* and *Yoga vashista*. On the order of his brother Aurangzeb, who ascended the throne after his father, Dara was executed in 1659 as a heretic because he stated in his book *Majma ul Bahrayn* ("the meeting of two oceans", referring to Hinduism and Islam) that the Koran meant to indicate the Vedic texts when it spoke of the *Kitab al Maknun*, "the hidden book".

In Europe, after the cultural darkness of the middle ages, the French illuminists were among the first to rediscover the fascination for the ancient Indian wisdom. Voltaire (1694-1774) wrote, "The Vedas are the most precious gift for which the west is eternally indebted to the east... everything came to us from the banks of the Ganges - astronomy, astrology, metempsychosis and so on. It is important to note that at least 2500 years ago Pythagoras traveled from Samo to the Ganges to learn geometry. Certainly he would not have embarked in such a journey if the reputation of the *brahmanas'* science had not been established in Europe for a long time."

A contemporary of Voltaire, Pierre Sonnerat (1748-1814), author or *Voyage to the east Indies and China*, wrote, "Among the Indians we find the traces of the remotest antiquity... we know that all peoples came here to seek the elements of their knowledge... It is well known that Pythagoras went to India to study under the *brahmanas*, who were the most enlightened among the human beings... In her splendor, India gave religion and law to all the other peoples; Egypt and Greece owed her their own wisdom."

Astronomer Jean-Claude Bailly (1736–1793), member of the Academy of Sciences, wrote, "The Hindu astronomical system is much more ancient than the ones of the Greeks and even of the Egyptians; the calculations made by the Hindus 4500 years ago on the star movements are precise to the minute." Another French astronomer, Pierre Simon de Laplace (1749-1827), who became famous for his hypothesis on the origin of the solar system from a nebula, as well as for the equation and the mathematical differential operator that took his name, wrote, "It is India that gave us the ingenuous method to express all numbers with 10 symbols, each with a value of position and an absolute value - a deep and important idea that only seems so simple now because we ignore its true merit. This simplicity, this ease of utilization that conferred to all calculations, puts our arithmetics above all other useful inventions. We can better appreciate the greatness of this conquest when we remember that it escaped the genius of Archimedes and Apollinius, two of the greatest men produced by antiquity."

Abraham Hyacinthe Anquetil-Duperron (1731-1805) was the first academic scholar to study specifically Indian culture. He lived in India for 7 years and produced the French translation of the *Zenda Avesta*, the main text of parsism, and also a Latin translation of the *Upanishads* published in 1804, that became one of Arthur Schopenhauer's favorite readings.

Duperron wrote, "If the British... continue to refuse to enrich European culture with the Sanskrit scriptures... they will bear the shame of having sacrificed honor, honesty and humanity to the vile lust for gold and money, and man's knowledge will get no glory or benefit from their conquests."

Another French thinker of the times, Victor Cousin (1792-1867), wrote, "By carefully reading the poetic and philosophical monuments of the East, and especially of India, that are starting to spread in Europe, we discover so many and so deep truths, that we are compelled to kneel in front of eastern philosophy, and to see this cradle of the human race as the motherland of the most sublime philosophy."

Cousin, too, became a source of inspiration for the subsequent generations, among which we may mention Théodore Simon Jouffroy, Jean Philibert Damiron, Garnier, Pierre-Joseph Proudhon, Jules Barthelemy Saint-Hilaire, Felix Ravaisson-Mollien, Charles de Rémusat, Ralph Waldo Emerson, Jules Simon, Paul Janet, Adolphe Franck and Patrick Edward Dove.

In France the interest for the study of the *Vedas* continued with Jules Michelet (1798-1874), who wrote, "From India we get a stream of light, a river of Right and Reason... while in our West dry and barren minds treat Nature with arrogance, the Indian spirit, that is the richest and most fecund of all, has generously embraced universal brotherhood, that includes the identity of all souls."

Another great Frenchman, Victor Hugo (1802-1885), author of *Les miserables* and *Notre Dame de Paris*, wrote a poem on *Kena Upanishad*.

Henri Frédéric Amiel (1821- 1881) stated, "It is not a bad thing, to have some brahminical souls in the western world."

Paul Verlaine (1844-1896) wrote a poem entitled after Savitri and considered the Vedic texts "much better than the Bible, the Gospels and all the works written by the Fathers of the Church."

Romain Rolland (1866-1944), Nobel Prize 1915 for literature, author of a book on Ramakrishna's life, added, "If there is a place on this earth where man's dream have found a home since the earliest days of his existence, this is India! For over 30 centuries the tree of vision, with all its thousands of branches and millions of twigs, has grown in this torrid land, the burning lap of the Gods, and is tirelessly renovated... Let us return to our eagle nest on the Himalaya. It is waiting for us because it belongs to us, and we, european eaglets, do not need to renounce any part of our true nature... The spirit of the Vedanta has never been obstructed by a class of priests, each man has been totally free to go wherever he wanted, seeking the spiritual explanation for the spectacle of the universe."

The Frenchman Edgar Quinet (1803-1875) was the first to introduce the concept of "eastern renaissance... a new reform of the religious and secular world: this is the great subject of today's philosophy."

Followed Pierre Loti (1850-1923, *nom de plume* of Louis-Marie-Julien Viaud) who wrote, "I pay homage to you with veneration and awe, o ancient India, of whom I am an adept, India of the greatest glory of arts and philosophy... May your awakening dazzle the west!"

Edward Gibbon (1734-1794), great English historian of the Enlightenment period, author of the famous *The Decline and Fall of the Roman Empire,* describes with admiration the freedom of religion in Hinduism: "Thus the Hindus have an extraordinary wide selection of beliefs and practices to choose from: they can be monotheists, pantheists, polytheists, agnostics or even atheists. They may follow a strict or a loose standard of moral conduct, or they may choose instead an amoral emotionalism or mysticism. They may worship regularly at a temple or may not go there at all. ... The ancient Romans also had a similar form of worship like the Hindus... The policy of the emperors and the senate, as far as it concerned religion, was happily seconded by the enlightened, and by the habits of the superstitious, part of their subjects. The various modes of worship, which prevailed in the Roman world, were all considered by the people, as equally true; by the philosopher as equally false; and by the magistrate as equally useful. And thus toleration produced not only mutual indulgence, but even religious concord."

Among the other great British thinkers of the times, we may mention Percy Bysshe Shelley (1792-1822), who later became the idol of subsequent generations of poets such as Robert Browning, Alfred Tennyson, Dante Gabriel Rossetti, Algernon Charles Swinburne and William Butler Yeats. Both Shelley and his wife Mary (author of the famous *Frankenstein* novel) were passionate admirers of Vedic wisdom, that also turned them into vegetarian activists. Shelley even wanted to move to India. Robert Southey (1774-1843) was the first English poet to incorporate Vedic references in his works - for example in *The curse of Kehama* he speaks of mount Meru, Parvati, Shiva and the Ganges.

Among the German admirers of Vedic knowledge we can mention Immanuel Kant (1712-1804), who gave many lectures on the subject at the Konigberg University in eastern Prussia, and Johann Gottfried Herder (1744-1803) the leader of the famous movement Sturm und Drang. He wrote, "(India is) the lost paradise of all the religions and philosophies, the cradle of humanity, and my eternal home, the great Orient awaiting to be discovered within ourselves. The origins of mankind can be traced back to India, where the human mind has obtained the first forms of wisdom and virtue with a simplicity, a strength and a sublimity that have, frankly, absolutely no equal in our cold philosophical european world."

A very similar opinion was expressed by Friedrich Creuzer (1771-1858), philologist and archeologist, in his *Symbolik und Mythologie der allen Volker*: "If there is a country on earth which can justly claim the honor of having been the cradle of the human race or at least the scene of the earliest civilization, the successive developments of which carried into all parts of the ancient world and even beyond, the blessings of knowledge which is the second life of man, that country assuredly is India."

August Wilhelm von Schlegel (1767-1845) founder of the Romantic movement together with his brother Frederich (1772-1829), produced 18 lectures on *Bhagavad gita*, entitled *Dialogues of Krishna and Arjoon*. In his commentaries he wrote, "Even the loftiest philosophy of the Europeans, the idealism of reason as it is set forth by the Greek philosophers, appears in comparison with the abundant light and vigor of Oriental idealism like a feeble Promethean spark in the full fold of heavenly glory of the noonday sun, faltering and feeble and ever ready to be extinguished."

The Prussian minister of public education, Wilhelm von Humboldt (1767-1835) became such an enthusiast of Schlegel's edition of *Bhagavad gita* that he started to study Sanskrit himself.

He wrote to his friend, the statesman Frederick von Gentz (1764-1832): "I read the Indian poem for the first time when I was in my country estate in Silesia and, while doing so, I felt a sense of overwhelming gratitude to God for having let me live to be acquainted with this work. It must be the most profound and sublime thing to be found in the world."

Friedrich Majer (1771-1818) wrote, "It will no longer remain to be doubted that the priests of Egypt and the sages of Greece have drawn directly from the original well of India... Towards the Orient, to the banks of the Ganga and the Indus that our hearts feel drawn as by some hidden urge - it is there that all the dark presentiments point which lie in the depths of our heart...In the Orient, the heavens poured forth into the earth."

In his book *Philosophy of Mythology*, F. W. J. Schelling (1773-1854) devoted over 100 pages to India; in a 1802 lecture he praised "the sacred texts of the Indians, that are superior to the Bible."

Novalis (1772-1801), pseudonym of Baron Friedrich von Hardenberg, leader of the romantic movement, wrote, "Sanskrit takes me back to the original people that had been forgotten."

Inspired by von Schlegel, Friedrich Ruckert (1788-1866), professor of eastern languages in Erlangen from 1827 to 1841, produced many translations from Sanskrit to German, including the *Gita Govinda*.

Henrich Heine (1797-1856), whose poems were put in music as Lieder ("sonate") by Robert Schumann and Franz Schubert, speaks in his Buch der Lieder "the dear motherland, the blue and sacred Ganga, the eternally shining Himalayas, the gigantic forests of Banyan trees on whose wide shadowy paths quietly walk wise elephants and pilgrims".

Always in the field of music, it is interesting to know that Ludwig van Beethoven (1770-1827) left several fragments of translations and adaptation of the *Upanishads* and *Bhagavad gita*.

However, the most famous scholar of the Vedas in this period was Arthur Schopenhauer (1788-1860), who wrote, "There is no religion or philosophy so sublime and elevating as Vedanta... The Vedas are the most rewarding and the most elevating book which can be possible in the world... In the whole world there is no study so beneficial and so elevating as that of the Upanishads. It is destined sooner or later to become the faith of the people... It has been the solace of my life - it will be the solace of my death. It is the product of the highest human wisdom." Schopenhauer openly expressed his disappointment about the european Christian culture based on the Bible; he often proclaimed that his own philosophy was based on Vedic teachings.

Another great German scholar, Johann Wolfgang von Goethe (1749-1832), expressed in various occasions his admiration for the works of Kalidasa (*Shakuntala* and *Meghaduta*) and for *Gita Govinda*.

Heinrich Zimmer (1890-1943), the greatest German scholar on Indian philology, to whom a Chair was dedicated at the University of Heidelberg (for Indian philosophy and intellectual history), wrote, "with the cult of the Great Goddess in Hinduism, the archaic heritage of sensual earth-bound rites rises once again overwhelmingly to the zenith".

Friedrich Nietzsche (1844-1900) spoke disparagingly of those Europeans who, lacking in intellectual discernment, wanted to convert and "civilize" the *brahmanas*. Paul Dessen (1845-1919) also known as Deva Sena, wrote, "on the tree of wisdom there is no fairer flower than the Upanishads, and no finer fruit than the Vedanta philosophy".

Carl Gustav Jung (1875-1961), the founder of the Analythical Psychology, gave summer lectures on yoga philosophy and kundalini in Zurich for a few years. He wrote, "We do not yet realize that while we are turning upside down the material world of the East with our technical proficiency, the East with its psychic proficiency, is throwing our spiritual world into confusion."

Rudolph Steiner (1861-1925), the famous founder of the Anthroposofic Society, wrote, "What we read in the Vedas, those archives of Hindu wisdom, gives us only a faint idea of the sublime doctrines of the ancient teachers".

Herman Hesse (1877-1962), Nobel Prize 1946 for literature, became famous for his *Siddharta*, a novel centered on spiritual search in ancient India. He wrote, "India is not only a country and something geographical, but the home and the youth of the soul, the everywhere and nowhere, the oneness of all times... The marvel of the Bhagavad-Gita is its truly beautiful revelation of life's wisdom which enables philosophy to blossom into religion."

Albert Einstein (1879-1995), famous physicist, author of the revolutionary relativity theory and the law of the photoelectrical effect (the basis of quanta theory) and Nobel Prize for Physics 1921, declared, "We owe a lot to Indians who taught us how to count, without which no worthwhile scientific discovery could have been made... When I read the Bhagavad-Gita and reflect about how God created this universe everything else seems so superfluous."

The Belgian Count Maurice di Maeterlinck (1862-1949), Nobel Prize 1911 for literature, explains in his book *Mountain Paths* that the doctrine of Karma is "the only satisfactory solution of life's injustices." He also wrote,

"We cannot tell how the religion of the Hindus came into being... we find it already complete in its broad outlines, its main principles. Not only is it complete, but the farther back we go, the more perfect it is, the more unadulterated..."

Georg Wilhelm Friedrich Hegel (1887-1961), one of the most famous German philosophers, author of the thesis of Total Reality, wrote, "India has created a special momentum in world history as a country to be searched for... Without being known too well, it has existed for millennia in the imagination of the Europeans as a wonderland. Its fame, which it has always had with regard to its treasures, both its natural ones, and in particular, its wisdom, has lured men there... India has always been an object of yearning, a realm of wonder, a world of magic."

Inspired by the ancient Indian schools described by the Greeks, Count Hermann Keyserling (1880-1946) founded in 1920 the *School of Wisdom* in Darmstadt, Germany - based on the concept of a planetary culture beyond nationalism and cultural ethnocentrism. He wrote abut the "absolute superiority of India over the West in philosophy; poetry from the Mahabharata, containing the Bhagavad-Gita, "perhaps the most beautiful work of the literature of the world."

One of the most remarkable personalities of this period was Margaret Elizabeth Noble (1867-1911), born in Ireland, but famous in India as Sister Nivedita. She wrote various books, such as *The Master as I Saw Him;*

Notes of Some Wanderings; Kedar Nath and Bhadri Narayan; Kali the Mother; The Web of Indian Life; An Indian Study of Love and Death; Studies from an Eastern Home; Indian Art; Cradle Tales of Hinduism; Religion and Dharma; Aggressive Hinduism; Footfalls of Indian History; Civic Ideal and Indian Nationality; Hints on National Education in India; Lambs Among Wolves; On Education; On Hindu Life, Thought and Religion; On Political, Economic and Social Problems. She met Swami Vivekananda in London in 1895 and became his disciple, moving to Calcutta on his invitation and accepting the order of *brahmacharya* in 1989; she the first western woman admitted to an Indian monastic order. A few weeks later she was joined by two more female disciples of Vivekananda, the Americans Sara C. Bull (wife of the famous Norwegian violinist and composer Ole Bull) and Josephine MacLeod. Vivekananda had written her, "Let me tell you frankly that I am now convinced that you have a great future in the work for India. What was wanted was not a man, but a woman - a real lioness - to work for Indians, women especially. India cannot yet produce great women, she must borrow them from other nations. Your education, sincerity, purity, immense love, determination and above all, the Celtic blood make you just the woman wanted."

She was intimate friend of Sarada Devi (Ramakrishna's wife), Aurobindo Ghosh and many intellectuals in the Bengali community, such as Rabindranath Tagore, Jagadish Chandra Bose (the Indian scientist that invented the radio simultaneously with Marconi) and his wife Abala Bose, and the artists Abanindranath Tagore, Ananda Coomaraswami and Nandalal Bose. She is particularly famous in India because she actively contributed to the cause of Indian independence and to the development of a Hindu educational system for women, including adult women and widows. She wrote, "The whole history of the world shows that the Indian intellect is second to none... Are the countrymen of Bhaskaracharya and Shankaracharya inferior to the countrymen of Newton and Darwin? We trust not."

In this brief review of the admirers of Indian culture we cannot forget the founders of the Theosophical Society. Helena Petrova Blavatsky (1831-1891) greatly drew from Vedic knowledge, especially from the *Upanishads* and the *Vedanta*, to write her *magnum opus*, *The Secret Doctrine* (published in 1885). It was precisely the Theosophians who first introduced Mohandas Karamchand Gandhi to the reading of *Bhagavad gita*.

The Theosophist Christopher W. B. Isherwood (1904-1986) worked with Swami Prabhavananda to the translation of *Gita*, *Upanishads* and Patanjali's *Yoga sutras*, awakening among Indians a new interest for vedic knowledge, "that was so valued by westerners". Isherwood also wrote Vedanta for the Western World and My Guru and His Disciple (about Swami Prabhavananda, who was his spiritual guide for about 30 years). He declared, "I believe the Gita to be one of the major religious documents of the world... The Gita is not simply a sermon, but a philosophical treatise."

Colonel Henry S Olcott (1832-1907), co-founder of the Theosophical Society together with Blavatsky, strongly believed that "the ancient Hindus could navigate the air, and not only navigate it, but fight battles in it... they must have known all the arts and sciences related to the science", as he stated in a lecture in Allahabad (the ancient Prayaga).

Probably the most famous personality in this Theosophist group was Annie Wood Besant (1847-1933), active socialist on the executive committee of the Fabian Society along with George Bernard Shaw. She became directly engaged in the Indian independence movement and was a founder of the Indian National Congress (still today the most powerful party on the Indian political scene). Besant wrote, "After a study of some forty years and more of the great religions of the world, I find none so perfect, none so scientific, none so philosophical and none so spiritual that the great religion known by the name of Hinduism. Make no mistake, without Hinduism, India has no future... This is the India of which I speak - the India which, as I said, is to me the Holy Land. For those who, though born for this life in a Western land and clad in a Western body, can yet look back to earlier incarnations in which they drank the milk of spiritual wisdom from the breast of their true mother - they must feel ever the magic of her immemorial past, must dwell ever under the spell of her deathless fascination; for they are bound to India by all the sacred memories of their past; and with her, too, are bound up all the radiant hopes of their future, a future which they know they will share with her who is their true mother in the soul-life... India is the mother of religion. In her are combined science and religion in perfect harmony, and that is the Hindu religion, and it is India that shall be again the spiritual mother of the world."

Mirra Alfassa (Morisset or Rochard, 1878-1973), also known as Mother Meera, or Mère as she was called by Aurobindo and his followers, arrived in India for the first time with Alexandra David-Neel (1868-1969), French explorer and scholar in Sanskrit and Buddhism at the Sorbonne University - the first woman to travel alone in India and to organize tours for her friends. In 1920 Mère settled in Pondicherry where she established an ashrama for Aurobindo, who had decided to retire in isolation. This first ashrama later developed into the great project now known as Auroville.

Also rather famous, albeit extremely controversial, is the Russian George Ivanovich Gurdjieff (1877-1949). Both Gurdjieff and his "rebellious" student Peter D. Ouspensky (1878-1947) greatly drew from the Indian traditions of Yoga and sacred dance to create their personal philosophy, although they never recognized their intrinsic original value. In this, they were following the path already traced by the medieval sufis, dervishes and fakirs, that had come in touch with the surviving fragments of the Hellenic and Vedic knowledge and utilized some of their concepts to build an "islamic mysticism" to mellow out the public image of the political Islam.

The number of the admirers of Vedic knowledge continued to grow all over Europe among philosophers, literates, scientists, musicians and thinkers of all fields. Here is a brief chronological list.

Edward Washburn Hopkins (1857-1932), American sanskritist who studied at Leipzig, secretary of the American Oriental Society and director of its magazine, and also author of several books, such as *Religions of India, Epic Mythology, History of Religions, Origin and Evolution of Religion*.

Goldsworthy Lowes Dickinson (1862-1932), pacifist activist during World War 1, was the father of the concept of the League of Nations, that later became the United Nations Organization. Hailing from a Christian-socialist family, Dickinson gave up Christianity and embraced the Indian religion. *In An Essay on the Civilizations of India, China & Japan*, he wrote, "The real antithesis is not between East and West, but between India and the rest of the world. Only India is different; only India unspools some other possibility fantastically.. In the first place, India has never put Man in the center of the universe. In India, and wherever Indian influence has penetrated, it is, on the one hand, the tremendous forces of nature, and what lies behind them that is the object of worship and of speculation; and, on the other hand, Mind and Spirit; not the mind or spirit of the individual person, but the universal Mind or Spirit, which is in him, but which he can only have access by philosophic mediation and discipline... Indian religion has never been a system of dogma, and is not entangled in questionable history. Indian philosophy and religion have always affirmed that there is; that by meditation and discipline an internal perception is opened which is perception of truth."

Gustav Holst (1874-1934) composed various symphonies inspired by the Hindu scriptures: in 1903 to Indra and in 1908 to Savitri (inspired by the *Mahabharata* episode) and *The Cloud Messenger*, inspired by Kalidasa's *Meghaduta*. Another work, dedicated to Sita and inspired by the *Ramayana*, was never completed. Later in life he started to study Sanskrit to produce a translation of the *Rig Veda* that could be adapted to western music.

Lady Maria Callcott (1785-1842) also known as Mrs. Graham, from the name of her second husband. She is the author of *Journal of a Residence in India*, published in 1812 when she returned to England. She declared that the purpose of her journal was "'to exhibit a sketch of India's former grandeur and refinement so that I could restore India to that place in the scale of ancient nations, which European historians have in general unaccountably neglected to assign to it... Were all other monuments swept away from the face of Hindustan, were all its inhabitants destroyed, and its name forgotten, the existence of the Sanskrit language would prove that it once contained a race who had reached a high degree of refinement... superior to the havoc of war and conquest, it remains a venerable monument of the splendour of other times, as the solid Pyramid in the deserts of Egypt."

Albert Schweizer (1875-1965) wrote, "The Bhagavad-Gita has a profound influence on the spirit of mankind by its devotion to God which is manifested by actions."

Erwin Schroedinger (1887-1961), Austrian physicist and political refugee, Nobel Prize 1933 for quantum mechanics, kept at his bedside *Gita*, *Upanishads*, and various Vedic texts especially on Yoga and Sankhya. He stated, "Some blood transfusion from the East to the West to save Western science from spiritual anemia... is the only solution... found in the ancient wisdom of the Upanishads." Schroedinger was the author of *What is Life? The Physical Aspect of the Living Cell*, and *Mind and Matter*, both inspired by Vedic concepts. Especially the second book became very famous and according to Francis Clark, who discovered the DNA genetic code, it created the basis for that revolutionary breakthrough. Here are some extracts, "This life of yours which you are living is not merely a piece of this entire existence, but in a certain sense the whole; only this whole is not so constituted that it can be surveyed in one single glance. This, as we know, is what the Brahmins express in that sacred, mystic formula which is yet really so simple and so clear; tat tvam asi, this is you... From the great Upanishads the recognition Atman = Brahman was considered, far from being blasphemous, to represent, the quintessence of deepest insight into the happenings of the world. The striving of all the scholars of Vedanta was, after having learnt to pronounce with their lips, really to assimilate in their minds this grandest of all thoughts."

According to Schroedinger's biographer, Walter Moore, "The unity and continuity of Vedanta are reflected in the unity and continuity of wave mechanics. In 1925, the world view of physics was a model of a great machine composed of separable interacting material particles. During the next few years, Schrodinger and Heisenberg and their followers created a universe based on super imposed inseparable waves of probability amplitudes. This new view would be entirely consistent with the Vedantic concept."

Friedrich Heiler (1892-1967), author of *Mysticism of the Upanishads, Christian faith and Indian thought* and *Das Gebet and Die Religionen der Menschheit*, wrote, "India is our motherland of speculative theology... There runs an unbroken chain from the Atman-Brahman mysticism of the Vedic Upanishads to the Vedanta of Sankara on the one side and on the other through the mystical technique of the Yoga system... Another line of development equally continuous leads from the Orphic-Dionysiac mysticism to Plato, Philo and the later Hellenistic mystery cults to the Neoplatonic mysticism of the Infinite of Plotinus which is in turn is the source of the mystical theology" of the pseudo-Dionysius the Areioagute. Perhaps this second chain is only an offshoot from the first."

Amos Bronson Alcott (1799-1888), self-taught philosopher and school teacher, strictly vegetarian and founder of the community "Fruitlands", was author of *Orphic Sayings, Tablets*, and *Concord Days*. He was the father of Louisa and May Alcott, famous respectively as a writer and an artist. Ralph Waldo Emerson was so impressed by Amos' intellectual power that he convinced him to move to Concord and join his circle of friends. Amos wrote in his diary, "I read more of the Bhagavad Gita and felt how surpassingly fine were the sentiments. These, or selections from this book should be included in a Bible for Mankind... Were I a preacher, I would venture sometimes to take from its texts the motto and moral of my discourse. It would be healthful and invigorating to breathe some of this mountain air into the lungs of Christendom."

Ralph Waldo Emerson (1803-1882), father of the American Transcendentalist Movement, writer, philosopher, minister of the Unitarian Church, lecturer and professor of theology at Harvard, was a great admirer of Vedic scriptures. He came to know about the Vedic texts from the works of Victor Cousin, and from his 1845 diary we learn that he was reading *Bhagavad gita* and Henry Thomas Colebrooke's *Essays on the Vedas*. We also know he read the *Vishnu Purana*, *Katha Upanishad* and various other texts. Emerson wrote, "I owed a magnificent day to the Bhagavad-Gita. It was as if an empire spoke to us, nothing small or unworthy, but large, serene, consistent, the voice of an old intelligence which in another age and climate had pondered and thus disposed of the same questions which exercise us.... When Confucius and the Indian Scriptures were made known, no claim to monopoly of ethical wisdom could be thought of. It is only within this century (in the 1800s) that England and America discovered that their nursery tales were old German and Scandinavian stories; and now it appears that they came from India, and are therefore the property of all the nations... (Vedic thought) is sublime as night and a breathless ocean. It contains every religious sentiment, all the grand ethics which visit in turn each noble poetic mind.... Nature makes a Brahmin of me presently: eternal compensation, unfathomable power, unbroken silence.... Peace, she saith to me, and purity... It teaches to speak truth, love others, and to dispose trifles... all is soul and the soul is Vishnu ... Hari is always gentle and serene."

In his poem *Brahman*, Emerson offers the perspective of American Vedantism, and in his Essays we find many comments on Vedic knowledge and its diffusion in the West. Among his other poems on Vedic knowledge, we may mention *Hamatreya* and *Maya*.

John Greenleaf Whittier (1807-1892), one of Emerson's circle of friends, borrowed a copy of the *Bhagavad gita* from him and wrote, "It is a wonderful book-and has greatly excited my curiosity to know more of the religious literature of the East." He later introduced many vedic ideas in his poems, including *The Brewing of Soma*, that imaginatively describes the use of the Vedic sacrificial drink.

Another representative of American Transcendentalist, Walt Whitman (1813-1892), is the author of the famous *Leaves of Grass*, and *Passage to India*. In another poem, entitled *Salut Au Monde*, he wrote, "I hear the

Hindoo teaching his favorite pupil he loves, wars, adages, transmitted safely to this day from poets who wrote three thousand years ago."

Emerson described *Leaves of Grass* as something between the *Gita* and the *New York Tribune Herald.* In his 1889 essay *A Backward Glance O'er Travel'd Roads*, Whitman says he read "the ancient Hindu poems".

Henry David Thoreau (1817-1862), also part of Emerson's circle, was a philosopher, writer, social critic and the father of the "civil disobedience" concept. Although he was a minister of the Unitarian Church, he rejected organized Christianity (he never went to church) and wrote, "Whenever I have read any part of the Vedas, I have felt that some unearthly and unknown light illuminated me. In the great teaching of the Vedas, there is no touch of sectarianism.... When I read it, I feel that I am under the spangled heavens of a summer night... In the morning I bathe my intellect in the stupendous and cosmogonal philosophy of the Bhagavat Geeta, since whose composition years of the gods have elapsed, and in comparison with which our modern world and its literature seem puny and trivial... I would say to the readers of the Scriptures, if they wish for a good book, read the Bhagvat-Geeta... It deserves to be read with reverence even by Yankees... Ex oriente lux may still be the motto of scholars, for the Western world has not yet derived from the East all the light it is destined to derive thence... One sentence of the Gita, is worth the State of Massachusetts many times over."

From 1849 to 1855 he borrowed all the Indian texts of the library of Harvard University, and in 1855 he received from his friend Thomas Chilmondeley a gift of 44 eastern volumes, including *Rig Veda Samhita, Mandukya Upanishad, Vishnu Purana, Manu smriti, Bhagavad gita,* and *Bhagavata Purana.*

Herman Melville (1819-1891), author of the novel *Moby Dick*, wrote, "the most ancient extant portrait anyways purporting to the whale's is to be found in the famous cavern pagoda of Elephanta, in India. ...The Hindoo whale referred to, occurs in a separate department of the wall, depicting the incarnation of Vishnu in the form of leviathan, learnedly known as the Matse-Avatar."

Lev Nikolaevich Tolstoy (1828-1910), Russian writer and mystic, founder of the first vegetarian society (closed down in 1917 by the bolshevic revolution) quoted in a 1909 letter to Gandhi the *Upanishads, Bhagavad gita* and the Tamil *Tirukkural*, as well as Vivekananda's writing, encouraging Indians "not to give up their ancient religious culture for the materialism of the West."

He inserted many quotes from the Vedas in his *Range of Reading, Thoughts of Wise Men*, and other collections. To the orthodox Church that informed him about his excommunication, he replied, "To regard Christ as God, and to pray to him, are to my mind the greatest possible sacrilege."

Sir Edwin Arnold (1832-1904), wrote a translation of *Bhagavad gita* entitled *The Song Celestial.* He wrote in the introduction, "This famous and marvelous Sanskrit poem... enjoys immense popularity and authority in India, where it is reckoned as one of the "Five Jewels" - pancharatnani - of Devanagari literature... blending as it does the doctrine of Kapila, Patanjali, and the Vedas." In his book India Revisited he emotionally describes the ritual of ablutions in the Ganges river.

Mark Twain is the pen name of Samuel Langhorne Clemens (1835-1910). One of the most famous American writers, he is the author of *The Adventures of Huckleberry Finn, The Adventures of Tom Sawyer, A Connecticut Yankee in King Arthur's Court, Following the Equator* and *Travelogue* - a sort of diary on his experiences in Asia.

He wrote, "Land of religions, cradle of human race, birthplace of human speech, grandmother of legend, great grandmother of tradition. The land that all men desire to see and having seen once even by a glimpse, would not give that glimpse for the shows of the rest of the globe combined... Our most valuable and most artistic materials in the history of man are treasured up in India only!.. India had the start of the whole world in the beginning of things. She had the first civilization; she had the first accumulation of material wealth; she was populous with deep thinkers and subtle intellects; she had mines, and woods, and a fruitful soul... Varanasi or Banaras is older than history, older than tradition, older even than legend, and looks twice as old as all of them put together."

Clarence Edward Dutton (1841-1912), geologist, poet and captain of the United States army, named the peaks of the Grand Canyon "Vishnu temple", "Shiva temple", and "Brahma temple".

Georg Morris Cohen Brandes (1842-1927), Danish literary critic, had a great influence on scandinavian literature. He wrote, "my spiritual home is on the banks of the Ganga."

William James (1842-1910), first president of the American Society for Psychical Research, philosopher and pioneer of psychology in America, brother to novelist Henry and diarist Alice. He was a close associate of Ralph Waldo Emerson, Charles Sanders Pierce, Bertrand Russell, Mark Twain, Henri Berson and Sigmund Freud. He wrote, "from the Vedas we learn a practical art of surgery, medicine, music, house building under which mechanized art is included. They are encyclopedia of every aspect of life, culture, religion, science, ethics, law, cosmology and meteorology."

Mihai Eminescu (1850-1889), the greatest Romanian poet, discovered Indian philosophy through Schopenhauer. In his poem *Tattvamasi* he speaks of the identity of Atman and Brahman. In another poem, *Kamadeva*, he speaks of the Deva of erotic love as the spark of creation.

Ella Wheeler Wilcox (1850-1919), American poet and journalist, supporter of the Rosicrucian movement in the United States, wrote, "India - the land of Vedas, the remarkable works contains not only religious ideas for a perfect life, but also facts which science has proved true. Electricity, radium, electronics, airship, all are known to the seers who founded the Vedas."

Richard Garbe (1857-1927), professor at the University of Tubingen, became famous for his work to trace the original version of *Bhagavad gita*. In 1885 he traveled to India on the request of the Ministry of Culture of the Prussian government, and later he published the diary of his experience under the title *Indian Travel Sketches*. This book is particularly interesting because in the 19th century very few German indologists actually visited India. He dedicated most of his life to study the Sankhya philosophy.

George Bernard Shaw, (1856-1950), Irishman, Nobel Prize 1925 for literature, vegetarian activist, socialist activist, founder of the London School of Economics, member of the Executive Committee of the Fabian Society, writer and dramatist, wrote, "The Indian way of life provides the vision of the natural, real way of life."

William Butler Yeats (1856-1939), another Irishman and Nobel Prize 1923 for literature, was a personal friend of Rabindranath Tagore, Mohini Chatterji and Sri Purohit Swami. He wrote a poem entitled to Mount Meru, which he identifies with the Everest, and where he pictures the yogis engaged in meditation.

He wrote, "It was my first meeting with a philosophy that confirmed my vague speculations and seemed at once logical and boundless."

Nicola Tesla (1856-1943), one of the most ingenuous inventors of western history, used Sanskrit terms such as *akasha* and *prana* to describe the natural phenomena and described the universe as a kinetic system full of energy that could be channeled from any point.

Alfred North Whitehead (1861-1947), pacifist activist, pioneer of mathematical logic and analythic philosophy, member of the Royal Society and the British Academy, president of the Aristotelian Society from 1922 to 1923, co-author with Bertrand Russell of the famous *Principia Mathematica*, stated, "Vedanta is the most impressive metaphysics the human mind has conceived."

Maurice Winternitz (1863-1937), famous indologist and author of *History of Indian Literature*, wrote, "From the mystical doctrines of the Upanishads, one current of thought may be traced to the mysticism of Persian Sufism, to the mystic, theosophic logos doctrine of the Neo-Platonics and the Alexandrian Christian Mystics, Eckhart and Tauler, and finally to the philosophy of the great German mystic of the nineteenth century, Schopenhauer... Garbe, the greatest authority on Samkhya Philosophy in Europe, has made it very probable that Samkhya Philosophy has been of influence on the philosophical ideas of Heraklitos, Empedokles, Anaxagoras, Demokritos and Epikuros... It seems to me to be proved the Pythagoras was influenced by the Indian Samkhya. Nor have I any doubt that the Gnostic and Neo-Platonic philosophies have been influenced by Indian philosophical ideas."

Sylvain Levi (1863-1935), French orientalist and professor of Sanskrit at the Sorbonne University, wrote, " From Persia to the Chinese sea, from the icy regions of Siberia to Islands of Java and Borneo, India has propagated her beliefs, her tales, and her civilization... has left indelible imprints on one fourth of the human race in the course of a long succession of centuries. She has the right to reclaim... her place amongst the great nations summarizing and symbolizing the spirit of humanity."

Rudyard Kipling (1865-1936), Nobel Prize 1907 for literature, author of the famous *The Jungle Book, Kim, Captains Courageous*, and *The Man Who Would Be King*. Among his poems the most famous are *Gunga Din, Mandalaya* and *The White Man's Burden*, in which he describes, with an irony that may be invisible to the eyes of the fanatic supporters of european imperialism, the attitude of the British colonist that believes himself invested with the duty to "civilize" the rest of the world, sacrificing in the attempt himself and his own children to exile. Kipling's parents moved to India before his birth, but as demanded by the social convention of the times, they sent him to England to study when he was 5, alone with his little sister aged 3. Rudyard was permanently scarred by the cultural and emotional trauma of the shift from the colonial home in Bombay to the Lorne Lodge, the private hostel in the house of Captain Holloway at Portsmouth, where Rudyard and his sister Alice - together with other children of British settlers in India - were regularly mistreated and neglected. At the age of

16 he returned to India, where he started his writing career.

Count Louis Hamon (1866-1936), born in Ireland as William John Warner and also known as Cheiro, was a famous palmist and astrologer, whose clients included Mark Twain, Sarah Bernhardt, Mata Hari, Oscar Wilde, Grover Cleveland, Thomas Edison, the Prince of Wales, General Kitchener, William Gladstone, Bernard Shaw and Joseph Chamberlain. He wrote, "Looking back to the earliest days of the history of the known world, we find that the first linguistic records belong to the people under consideration, and date back to that far distant cycle of time known as the Aryan civilization. Beyond history we cannot go; but the monuments and cave temples of India, according to the testimony of archaeologists, all point to a time so far beyond the scant history at our disposal... Long before Rome or Greece or Israel was even heard of, the mountains of India point back to an age, of learning beyond, and still beyond. From the astronomical calculations that the figures in their temples represent, it has been estimated that the Hindu understood the Precession of the Equinoxes centuries before the Christian Era... and made the calculation that it took place once in every 25,870 years. The observation and mathematical precision necessary to establish such a theory has been the wonder and admiration of modern astronomers. They, with their modern knowledge and up-to-date instruments, are still quarrelling among themselves as to whether the precession, the most important feature in astronomy, takes place every 25,870 years or every 24,500 years."

Herbert George Wells (1866-1946), historian and novelist, author of *The Time Machine, A Short History of the World* and *Crux Ansata: An Indictment of the Roman Catholic Church*, wrote, "The history of India for many centuries had been happier, less fierce, and more dreamlike than any other history. In these favorable conditions, they built a character - meditative and peaceful and a nation of philosophers such as could nowhere have existed except in India."

A. E. George Russell (1867-1935), Irish nationalist, economist, leader of the movement for cooperation among Irish farmers, poet, essayist, painter and mystic, wrote, "Goethe, Wordsworth, Emerson, and Thoreau among moderns have something of this vitality and wisdom but we can find all they have said and much more in the grand sacred books of India. The Bhagavad Gita and the Upanishads contain such godlike fullness of wisdom on all things that I feel the authors must have looked with calm remembrance back through a thousand passionate lives, full of feverish strife for and with shadows, ere they could have written with such certainty of things which the soul feels to be sure."

W. Somerset Maugham (1874-1965), son of the British ambassador in Paris, had an early start in his writing career and is considered the greatest English novelist. In India he met Ramana Maharshi - this event inspired his famous novel *The Razor's Edge*, whose title is taken from an example in *Katha Upanishad*: "the wise say that the path is like the sharp edge of the razor, narrow and difficult to tread". The main character in the story goes to India to seek relief from the horrors of the war and finds peace in the Indian philosophy of Vedanta.

Professor James Bissett Pratt (1875-1944), American writer author of *Why Religions Die* and *India and its Faiths*, believed that Hinduism was the only religion capable of surviving the modern crisis of faith. He wrote, "The Vedic Way.. is a self perpetuating religion... not death, but development... keeping that which in it was vital and true cast off the old shell and clothed itself in more suitable expression, with no break in the continuity of life and no loss in the sanctity and weight of its authority... If a religion is to live it must adapt itself to new and changing conditions; if it is to feed the spiritual life of its children, it must have the sensitivity and inventiveness that shall enable it to modify their as their needs demand... because of its ingrained conclusiveness, its tolerance, and its indifference to doctrinal divergences, stressed the essential unity of all Indian Dharmas, whether Hindu or Buddhist, and minimized differences... For most Westerners the histories of philosophy begin with the Greeks and end with the Americans, and convey not the least suggestion that anyone outside of the West ever had a philosophical idea. A glance at the curricula of most our colleges and universities would seem to indicate that the one principle on which they are planned might be phrased: nothing east of Suez!... To one who has had a taste of the riches which Indian thought and Indian literature can contribute to our intellectual life and our spiritual experience, this deprivation which we Westerners inflict upon ourselves and upon our young people seems pitiful in the extreme. Indian philosophical literature, taking its rise several centuries before the time of Thales, has swept down through the ages, retaining always a characteristic point of view of its own, but developing in a great variety of fresh forms. Indian thought constitutes today the one type of living philosophy independent of our Western tradition... The tendency of nearly all the schools of Western philosophy is more and more steadily setting in the direction of naturalism, and often of a rather crude naturalism. The victories of natural science have hypnotized most of our philosophers. From such a world as Western naturalism usually offers, the thoughtful mind which craves something more than a scientific pattern of space-time evens may be glad to take refuge in the eternal insights into a spiritual realm, spread out before us in the Upanishads, the Bhagavad-Gita, and the Vedantic philosophy."

Robert Earnest Hume (1877-1948), born in India from an American family, taught both in India and at Oxford. In 1921 he published *Thirteen Principal Upanishads*, in which he wrote, "In the long history of man's endeavor to grasp the fundamental truths of being, the metaphysical treatises known as the Upanishads hold an honored place . . . they are replete with sublime conceptions and with intuitions of universal truth... The

Upanishads undoubtedly have great historical and comparative value, but they are also of great present-day importance... The earnestness of the search for the Truth is one of the more delightful and commendable features of the Upanishads."

Jacob Wilhelm Hauer (1881-1961), the son of German protestant missionaries, taught in a missionary school in India from 1907 onwards. After coming in touch with Hinduism and yoga, he studied Sanskrit and wrote various books on the subject, such as *Der Yoga als Heilweg* ("Yoga as a means of salvation") dedicated to C.G. Jung. He considered *Bhagavad gita* as "a work of imperishable significance" occupying a central place in his own faith. He wrote, "gives us not only profound insights that are valid for all times and for all religious life, but it contains as well the classical presentation of one of the most significant phases of Indo-German religious history... It shows us the way as regards the essential nature and basal characteristics of Indo-Germanic religion."

Satyananda Stokes, born Samuel Evans Stokes (1882-1946), abandoned his studies at the Yale University at the age of 22 and traveled to India with the purpose of dedicating himself to the service of humanity. In 1905 he started working at a leper home at Sabathu, then he was sent to Kangra for rescue and relief work after a serious earthquake, and later he worked at the Christian Mission House at Kotgarh, in Himachal pradesh. In 1910 he purchased an abandoned tea plantation, he married and settled in Barubagh, Kotgarh. He built a temple for the Arya Samaj at Thanedar, which became famous as Paramajyoti Mandir, "the temple of the supreme Light". Although he still considered himself "a lover of Christ", he studied Sanskrit and in 1932 he officially became a Hindu in a ceremony performed by Arya Samaj. He expressed his own philosophy of life in a book entitled *Satyakam*, explaining that he had decided to convert to Hinduism because he detested the Christian concept of eternal punishment. He wrote, "The light from the Hindu scriptures had come to fill the gaps in Christianity."

Vera Christine Chute Collum (1883-1957), author of *The Dance of Civa or Life's Unity and Rhythm*, wrote, "The conviction that seeming diversities and differences are but passing and rhythmically varying phases of a fundamental unity led the East to symbolize Life and Death as the ever supple and continuously flowing Dance of Civa, in which construction and destruction are rhythmically pulsating patterns that the subtle dancer eternally presents and dissolves with the swiftness of a rapidly turning wheel."

Ernest E. Wood (1883-1965) lived in India for 38 years and founded 2 Universities, working as a principal and professor of physics, English and Sanskrit, with the aim of contributing to the Indian culture renaissance started by Rabindranath Tagore and his contemporaries. He was author of several books, including *Practical Yoga* and *The Glorious Presence*. He wrote, "Shankara did not leave the Vedanta teaching as a matter of religious belief, however, but said we must verify it by thinking, and the realize it by experience, as did the illumined men of old... The ancient Aryan thinkers who collected, collated, classified and commented upon the thought-traditions accumulated by their distant progenitors performed a rational and ethical service of the greatest value to posterity, when they put together a set of brief sayings, which they called the Vedanata (the end or highest point, of knowledge; the 'last word'), and presented them for study along with further statement: 'you will not be able to understand or realize the full import of these Great Sayings unless you first put your mind in order by certain practices or disciplines, which we will describe.'"

American writer Will Durant (1885-1981), author of *The Story of Philosophy, The Story of Civilization* (11 volume work for which he was awarded the Pulitzer Prize in 1967 and Presidential Medal of Freedom, by President Ford in 1977) and *The Case for India*, wrote, "India was the motherland of our race, and Sanskrit the mother of Europe's languages: she was the mother of our philosophy; mother, through the Arabs, of much of our mathematics; mother, through the village community, of self-government and democracy. Mother India is in many ways the mother of us all... It is true that even across the Himalayan barrier India has sent to us such questionable gifts as grammar and logic, philosophy and fables, hypnotism and chess, and above all our numerals and our decimal system. But these are not the essence of her spirit; they are trifles compared to what we may learn from her in the future... This is the India that patient scholarship is now opening up like a new intellectual continent to that Western mind which only yesterday thought civilization an exclusive Western thing."

General George S. Patton (1885-1945), one of the greatest military figures in history, came from a long family tradition in the army, firmly believed in reincarnation and was convinced that he had learned his personal strategic abilities on ancient battlefields. He often quoted *Bhagavad gita* to support his beliefs.

Rene Grousset (1885-1952), French historian, author of *Civilization of India* and *The Empire of the Steppes: A History of Central Asia*. He wrote, "In the high plateau of eastern Iran, in the oases of Serindia, in the arid wastes of Tibet, Mongolia, and Manchuria, in the ancient civilized lands of China and Japan, in the lands of the primitive Mons and Khmers and other tribes of Indo-China, in the countries of the Malaya-Polynesians, in Indonesia and Malay, India left the indelible impress of her high culture, not only upon religion, but also upon art, and literature, in a word, all the higher things of spirit... There is an obstinate prejudice thanks to which India is constantly represented as having lived, as it were, hermetically sealed up in its age-old civilization, apart from the rest of Asia. Nothing could be more exaggerated. During the first eight centuries of our era, so far as religion and art are concerned, central Asia was a sort of Indian colony. It is often forgotten that in the early Middle Ages there existed a 'Greater India,' a vast Indian empire... the Indian Ocean really deserved its name." Grousset was particularly impressed by Indian arts, and gave emotional descriptions of the images in the Elephanta caves and of Shiva Nataraja. In this regard he wrote, "Universal art has succeeded in few materialization of the Divine as powerful and also as balanced... Never have the overflowing sap of life, the pride of force superior to everything, the secret intoxication of the inner god of things been so serenely expressed."

Niels Bohr (1885-1962), Danish nuclear physicist, Nobel Prize 1922 for physics, wrote, "I enter the Upanishads to seek answers to my questions."

Leonard Bloomfield (1887-1949), American linguist, wrote, "The Hindu grammar taught Europeans to analyze speech forms; when one compared the constituent parts, the resemblances, which hitherto had been vaguely recognized, could be set forth with certainty and precision... As one of the greatest monuments of human intelligence is by no means an exaggeration; no one who has had even a small acquaintance with that most remarkable book could fail to agree. In some four thousand sutras or aphorisms - some of them no more than a single syllable in length - Panini sums up the grammar not only of his own spoken language, but of that of the Vedic period as well. The work is the more remarkable when we consider that the author did not write it down but rather worked it all out of his head, as it were. Panini's disciples committed the work to memory and in turn passed it on in the same manner to their disciples; and though the Astadhayayi has long since been committed to writing, rote memorization of the work, with several of the more important commentaries, is still the approved method of studying grammar in India today, as indeed is true of most learning of the traditional culture... It was in India, however, that there rose a body of knowledge which was destined to revolutionize European ideas about language."

T.S (Thomas Stearns) Eliot (1888-1965), poet and dramatist, Nobel Prize 1948 for literature, wrote, "Two years spent in the study of Sanskrit under Charles Lanman, and a year in the mazes of Patanjali's metaphysics under the guidance of James Woods, left me in a state of enlightened mystification. A good half of the effort of understanding what the Indian philosophers were after - and their subtleties make most of the great European philosophers look like schoolboys... In the literature of Asia is a great poetry... and I know that my own poetry shows the influence of Indian thought and sensibility."

Arnold Joseph Toynbee (1889-1975), author of *A Study of History*, an encyclopaedic work of metahistory or historical synthesis on the rise and fall of the various civilizations, with a strong spiritual orientation, wrote, "It is already becoming clear that a chapter which had a Western beginning will have to have an Indian ending if it is not to end in self-destruction of the human race. At this supremely dangerous moment in human history , the only way of salvation is the ancient Hindu way. Here we have the attitude and spirit that can make it possible for the human race to grow together in to a single family... So now we turn to India. This spiritual gift, that makes a man human, is still alive in Indian souls. Go on giving the world Indian examples of it. Nothing else can do so much to help mankind to save itself from destruction... India is not only the heir of her own religious traditions; she is also the residuary legatee of the Ancient Mediterranean World's religious traditions."

Walter Eidlitz (1892-1976), also known as Vaman dasa, author of *Journey to Unknown India*. He was a jew from Germany, and was sent to an internment camp during the World War 2 while he was traveling in search of God.

He later became a follower of the Gaudiya Vaishnava movement. He wrote, "God himself speaks the Bhagavad Gita, the innermost God which Brahma the Creator, Vishnu, the Preserver, and Shiva the Destroyer are only aspects."

Aldous Huxley (1894-1963), English novelist and essayist, author of *Brave New World, The Doors of Perception, Heaven and Hell* and *The Perennial Philosophy*, wrote, "The Bhagavad-Gita is the most systematic statement of spiritual evolution of endowing value to mankind. The Gita is one of the clearest and most comprehensive summaries of the spiritual thoughts ever to have been made... The Perennial Philosophy is expressed most succinctly in the Sanskrit formula, tat tvam asi ('That art thou'); the Atman, or immanent eternal Self, is one with Brahman, the

Absolute Principle of all existence; and the last end of every human being, is to discover the fact for himself, to find out who he really is."

Paul Brunton (1898-1981), traveler, mystic and author of *A Hermit in the Himalayas, A Message from Arunachala, The Orient: Legacy to the West*, and *A Search in Secret India*. His experience in India, among yogis, mystics and gurus culminates in his meeting with Ramana Maharshi in his ashram at Arunachala. He wrote, "We are witnessing in the West the appearance of an at present thin but slowly deepening current of interest in those very thoughts and ideas which the young men of India are today doing their best to reject as inadequate to their needs and which constitute the faith and religious traditions of their forefathers... The Bhagavad Gita contains the mental quintessence and successful synthesis of the various systems of religion and philosophy, it offers a unique epitome of the high culture of prehistoric India."

Theos Casimir Bernard (1908-1947), pioneer of the Indian and Tibetan studies at Columbia University, USA; his doctorate thesis was on Hatha Yoga. In his book *Hindu Philosophy* he wrote, "There is an innate in the human heart a metaphysical hunger to know and understand what lies beyond the mysterious and illusive veil of nature... Hindu philosophy does not attempt to train one to discern metaphysical truths; it offers a way of thinking which enables us one rationally to understand the reality experienced by self fulfilled personalities, and thereby to lead one to the realization of Truth. In this light, philosophy is seen as art of life and not a theory about the universe, for it is the means of attaining the highest aspirations of man. It is not for the discovery, but for the understanding of Truth."

David Bohm (1917-1992), one of the greatest physicists of quanta mechanics, pupil of Einstein and Oppenheimer, was deeply influenced by his contact with J. Krishnamurti. He wrote, "You would say Atman is more like the meaning. But then what is meant would be Brahman, I suppose; the identity of consciousness and cosmos."

Daniel Joseph Boorstin (1914-2004), American historian and Librarian of Congress from 1975 to 1987, author of *The Discovers, The Creators* and *The Seekers*. He wrote, "The Hindus have left an eloquent history of their efforts to answer the riddle of Creation. The Vedas, sacred hymns in archaic Sanskrit from about 1500 to 900 BC do not depict a benevolent Creator, but record a man's awe before the Creation as singers of the Vedas chant the radiance of this world. Their objects of worship were devas (cognate with Latin dues, god) derived from the old Sanskrit div, meaning brightness. Gods were the shining ones. The luminosity of their world impressed the Hindus from the beginning... What sanctifies the worshipper is no act of conversion, no change of spirit, but the simple act of seeing, the Hindi word darsan. A Hindu goes to a temple not to 'worship,' but rather for 'darshan,' to see the image of the deity... According to the Hindus, the deity or a holy spirit or place or image 'gives darsan' amd the people 'take darsan' for which there seems no counterpoint in any Western religion."

Joseph Campbell (1904-1987), author of *A Hero with Thousand faces*, was an intimate friend of J. Krishnamurti, and he cooperated to the translation of *The Gospel of Sri Ramakrishna*. He stated that the reading of *Mandukya Upanishad* had a stronger impact on him than the beginning of World War 2.

He wrote, "The first principle of Indian thought, therefore, is that the ultimate reality is beyond description. It is something that can be experienced only by bringing the mind to a stop; and once experienced, it cannot be described to anyone in terms of the forms of this world. The truth, the ultimate truth, that is to say, is transcendent. it goes past, transcends, all speech all images, anything that can possibly be said. But, as we have just seen, it is not only transcendent, it is also immanent, within all things, Everything in the world, therefore, is to be regarded as its manifestation... In the Biblical tradition, God creates man, but man cannot say that he is divine in the same sense that the Creator is, where as in Hinduism, all things are incarnations of that power. We are the sparks from a single fire. And we are all fire. Hinduism believes in the omnipresence of the Supreme God in every individual. There is no fall. Man is not cut off from the divine."

Ananda Kentish Coomaraswamy (1877-1947), originally from Sri Lanka, author of *The Dance of Shiva: Essays on Indian Art and Culture*, wrote, "We must, however, specially mention the Bhagavad Gita as probably the most important single work ever produced in India; this book of eighteen chapters is not, as it has been sometimes called, a "sectarian " work, but one universally studied and often repeated daily from memory by millions of Indians of all persuasions; it may be described as a compendium of the whole Vedic doctrine to be found in the earlier Vedas, Brahmanas, and Upanishads, and being therefore the basis of all the later developments, it can be regarded at the focus of all Indian religion."

Walter Raymond Drake (1913-1989), author of *Gods and Spacemen in the Ancient East*, published 4 years before Erich Von Daniken's bestseller *Chariots of the Gods*, wrote, "The oldest source of wisdom in the world must surely spring from India , whose initiates long ago probed the secrets of heaven, the story of Earth, the depths of Man's soul, and propounded those sublime thoughts which illumined the Magi of Babylon, inspired the philosophers of Greece and worked their subtle influence on the religions of the West... The Indian lyricize of spaceships faster than light and missiles more violent than H-bombs; their Sanskrit texts describe aircraft apparently with radar and cameras."

André Malraux (1901-1976), author of *Anti-memoir*, wrote, "The problem of this century is the religious problem and the discovery of Hindu thought will have a great deal to do with the solving of that particular problem."

John Archibald Wheeler (1911-2008), American theoretical physicist, worked with Niels Bohr on the foundations of nuclear fission, introduced the S-matrix and created the expressions *black hole, quantum foam* and *wormhole.* He wrote, "I like to think that someone will trace how the deepest thinking of India made its way to Greece and from there to the philosophy of our times."

Alun Lewis (1915-1944), who served in the military regiment of Royal Engineers in the World War 2, wrote *The Earth is a Syllable* - a story inspired by *Mandukya Upanishad* and that also contains a reference to the *Brihad aranyaka Upanishad.* The novel tells the story of a soldier who, mortally wounded in the jungle, experiences the various stages of awareness towards enlightenment and remembers the first verse of the *Mandukya Upanisad*: "the entire Earth is the syllable Om".

Yehudi Menuhin (1915-1999), one of the greatest violin players of the 20th century, descendent of Russian jews emigrated to America, became famous as disciple of the Hatha yoga teacher BKS Iyengar and friend of sitarist Ravi Shankar. He wrote, "India is the primal source, the mother country."

Nancy Wilson Ross (also known as Mrs. Stanley Young, 1901-1986), writer and lecturer, wrote, "Many hundreds of years before those great European pioneers, Galileo and Copernicus, had to pay heavy prices in ridicule and excommunication for their daring theories, a section of the Vedas known as the Brahmanas contained this astounding statement: The sun never sets or rises. When people think the sun is setting, he only changes about after reaching the end of the day and makes night below and day to what is on the other side. Then, when people think he rises in the morning, he only shifts himself about after reaching the end of the night."

Huston Smith (nato nel 1919), author of *The World's Religions, Science and Human Responsibility*, and *The Religions of Man*, wrote, "When I read the Upanishads, I found a profundity of world view that made my Christianity seem like third grade... The invisible excludes nothing, the invisible that excludes nothing is the infinite – the soul of India is the infinite."

Alexander Zinoviev (1922-2006), the controversial Russian writer and dissident intellectual, wrote, "But I would like to believe Hinduism is too valuable for humanity, and sacred Indian books contain too much precious and unique knowledge that it will not sink in oblivion. I'd like to believe that the principles of Indian philosophy and religion are much more in agreement with the needs for the future than any other religion in the world, in agreement with the tendency, known in Western countries as New Age. It's my deep belief that without India the world will sink in spiritual darkness and ignorance."

Carl Sagan (1934-1996), astrophysicist and author of *Cosmos*, wrote, "The Hindu religion is the only one of the world's great faiths dedicated to the idea that the

Cosmos itself undergoes an immense, indeed an infinite, number of deaths and rebirths. It is the only religion in which the time scales correspond, to those of modern scientific cosmology. Its cycles run from our ordinary day and night to a day and night of Brahma, 8.64 billion years long... And there are much longer time scales still."

Frithjof Schuon (1907-1998), author of *Language of the Self*, defined his own ideology as Sanatana Dharma, "the eternal religion", and wrote, "The Vedanta appears among explicit doctrines as one of the most direct formulations possible of that which makes the very essence of our spiritual reality."

Julius Robert Oppenheimer (1904-1967), famous as the "father of the atomic bomb", author of the Born-Oppenheimer approximation, the electron-positron theory, the Oppenheimer-Phillips process and the first foundations of the quantum tunneling, of the modern theory of neutrinic stars and black holes, quanta mechanics, the theory of the quantum field, and the interaction of the cosmic rays. He wrote, "What we shall find [in modern physics] is an exemplification, an encouragement, and a refinement of old wisdom... the juxtaposition of Western civilization's most terrifying scientific achievement with the most dazzling description of the mystical experience given to us by the Bhagavad Gita, India's greatest literary monument... the most beautiful philosophical song existing in any known tongue... Access to the Vedas is the greatest privilege this century may claim over all previous centuries."

Watching the first atomic explosion at the Trinity Test in New Mexico, on 16 July 1945, he emotionally quoted verse 11.12 of Gita: "If the radiance of a thousand suns Were to burst at once into the sky, That would be like the splendor of the Mighty One." He also quoted *Bhagavad gita* in a speech for the memorial service at the death of president Franklin D. Roosevelt. In 1963, the *Christian Century* magazine asked him in an interview to list the 10 books that did most to shape his vocational attitude and philosophy of life; he mentioned the *Bhagavad gita* (that he read in the original Sanskrit), Bhartrihari's *Satakatrayam*, and *The Waste Land* by T S Eliot, in which he speaks of the Vedic scriptures, specifically of the *Upanishads* and the *Gita.*

Queen Fredricka (1931-1981), researcher in physics and wife of King Paul of Greece, went to Kalahasti to pay homage to the Shankaracharya there, attracted by his book on the Advaita Vedanta. She declared, "While Greece is the country of my birth, India is the country of my soul."

Savitri Devi (1905-1982), born Maximiani Portas in France, obtained the Greek citizenship and embraced Hellenism, then she traveled to India to discover the roots of the aryan civilization and became famous in the nazi circles. She believes that only Hinduism could oppose the Judaeo-Christian heritage. In 1939 she published *A Warning to Hindus*, in which she expressed the fear that the Muslims could overtook the Hindus in India. In 1939 she married a Bengali *brahmana*, Asit Krishna Mukherjee; together they helped Subhash

Chandra Bose to get in touch with the Japanese to support his Indian National Army in the campaign against the British occupation. She wrote, "We defend Hinduism, because it is India's very self-expression; and we love India, because it is India... Hinduism is really superior to other religions, not for its spirituality, but for that still more precious thing it gives to its followers: a scientific outlook on religion and on life... If those of Indo-European race regard the conquest of pagan Europe by Christianity as a decadence, then the whole of Hindu India can be likened to a last fortress of very ancient ideals, of very old and beautiful religious and metaphysical conceptions, which have already passed away in Europe. Hinduism is thus the last flourishing and fecund branch on an immense tree which has been cut down and mutilated for two thousand years."

Werner Heisenberg (1901-1976), pioneer of quanta mechanics (formulated with Max Born and Pascual Jordan in 1925), father of the "uncertainty principle of quantum theory", Nobel Prize 1932 for the work that set the foundations for the discovery of the allotropic forms of hydrogen. At the end of the war he was appointed director of the Kaiser Wilhelm Institute for Physics and he reorganized it until the transfer to Munich in 1958, when it was renamed Max Planck Institute for Physics and Astrophysics. He was also president for the German Research Council, chairman of the Commission for Atomic Physics, chairman of the Nuclear Physics Working Group, and president of the Alexander von Humboldt Foundation. He wrote, "After the conversations about Indian philosophy, some of the ideas of Quantum Physics that had seemed so crazy suddenly made much more sense."

We must also mention Alain Danileou, Mircea Eliade and Juan Mascarò, respectively from France, Romania and Spain. Danielou (1907-1994, also known as Shiv Sharan), author of many books on the philosophy, religion, history and arts of India, such as *Virtue, Success, Pleasure, & Liberation : The Four Aims of Life in the Tradition of Ancient India*. He lived 15 years in India to study Sanskrit, he was initiated in Varanasi by Karpatraji Maharaja, and he was the first European to open claim to be a Hindu. He wrote, "The Hindu lives in eternity. He is profoundly aware of the relativity of space and time and of the illusory nature of the apparent world. Hinduism especially in its oldest, Shivaite form, never destroyed its past. It is the sum of human experience from the earliest times. Non-dogmatic, it allows every one to find his own way. The Greeks were always speaking of India as the sacred territory of Dionysus and historians working under Alexander the Greek clearly mentions chronicles of the Puranas as sources of the myth of Dionysus...The Egyptian myth of Osiris seemed directly inspired from a Shivaite story of the Puranas and that at any rate, Egyptians of those times considered that Osiris had originally come from India mounted on a bull (Nandi), the traditional transport of Shiva."

Eliade (1907-1986) novelist born in Bucharest, Romania; he was fluent in Romanian, French, German,

Italian and English, and could read Hebrew, Persian and Sanskrit. His long doctorate thesis was entitled *Yoga: Immortality and Freedom*, translated and published in French 3 years later. In 1928 he traveled to India, where he spent a long period studying at the University of Calcutta under the guidance of Surendranath Dasgupta, the author of a five volume *History of Indian Philosophy*. He wrote, "From the Upanishads onward, India has been seriously preoccupied with but one great problem - the structure of the human condition. With a rigor unknown elsewhere, India has applied itself to analyzing the various conditionings of the human being."

Mascarò (1897-1987) produced a translation of *Bhagavad gita*. He wrote, "Sanskrit literature is a great literature. We have the great songs of the Vedas, the splendor of the Upanishads, the glory of the Upanishads, the glory of the Bhagavad-Gita, the vastness (100,000 verses) of the Mahabharata, the tenderness and the heroism found in the Ramayana, the wisdom of the fables and stories of India, the scientific philosophy of Sankhya, the psychological philosophy of yoga, the poetical philosophy of Vedanta, the Laws of Manu, the grammar of Panini and other scientific writings, the lyrical poetry, and dramas of Kalidasa... The greatness of the Bhagavad Gita is the greatness of the universe, but even as the wonder of the stars in heaven only reveals itself in the silence of the night, the wonder of this poem only reveals itself in the silence of the soul.. the essence of the Bhagavad

Gita is the vision of God in all things and of all things in God."

Mascarò's work constitutes a remarkable exception to the deep ignorance and intellectual blindness shown by the scholars of Spain, Portugal and Italy, who remained largely unable to drop the prejudices of the colonial indology - as for example the Crepuscular Guido Gozzano (1883-1916) and the imaginative but disinformed Emilio Salgari (1862-1911). Also the more recent Antonio Tabucchi, Alberto Moravia and P.P. Pasolini have perceived India superficially and through dense prejudice, painting a sad picture of a miserable India, devoid of culture and humanity, doomed to remain slave to ignorant fatalism. Similarly, those who want to understand the genuine Indian tradition and the vedic wisdom may be misled by the famous novel *Passage to India* by Edward Morgan Forster, published for the first time in Great Britain in 1924 and by *The City of Joy* by Dominique Lapierre (both adapted for the big screen) and also by the recent movie *Slumdog millionaire*, directed by Danny Boyle.

Alan Watts (1915-1973), pioneer of the popularization of eastern knowledge in the 1960s, author of *The Way of Zen* and *Psychotherapy East and West*, wrote, "To the philosophers of India, however, Relativity is no new discovery, just as the concept of light years is no matter for astonishment to people used to thinking of time in millions of kalpas (a day of Brahma, about 4,320,000 earth years)."

Fritjof Capra (born in 1939), American of Austrian origin, founder of the *Center for Ecoliteracy* and author of *The Tao of Physics: An Exploration of the Parallels Between Modern Physics and Eastern Mysticism*, wrote, "Modern physics has shown that the rhythm of creation and destruction is not only manifest in the turn of the seasons and in the birth and death of all living creatures, but is also the very essence of inorganic matter. Modern physics has thus revealed that every subatomic particle not only performs an energy dance, but also is an energy dance; a pulsating process of creation and destruction... The dance of Shiva is the dancing universe, the ceaseless flow of energy going through an infinite variety of patterns that melt into one another... The scale of this ancient myth is indeed staggering; it has taken the human mind more than two thousand years to come up again with a similar concept... the two foundations of of twentieth-century physics - quantum theory and relativity theory - both force us to see the world very much in the way a Hindu, Buddhist...sees it."

Hans Torwesten (born in Germany in 1944), author of *Vedanta - Heart of Hinduism*, wrote, "A fair number of leading physicists and biologists have found parallels between modern science and Hindu ideas. In America, many writers such as J. D. Salinger (An Adventure in Vedanta: J.D. Salinger's the Glass Family), Henry Miller, Aldous Huxley, Gerald Heard, and Christopher Isherwood, were in contact with the Vedanta. Most of them came from elevated intellectual circles which rejected the dogmatism of the Christian Churches yet longed for spirituality and satisfactory answers to the fundamental questions of existence. In Vedanta, they found a wide-open, universal, and philosophically oriented religion where even the penetrating scientific mind could find something to its taste."

Canadian Klaus Klostermaier (born in 1933), Distinguished Professor in the Department of Religious Studies at the University of Manitoba in Canada and author of *Hinduism: A Short Introduction*, wrote, "Hinduism has proven much more open than any other religion to new ideas, scientific thought, and social experimentation. Many concepts like reincarnation, meditation, yoga and others have found worldwide acceptance. It would not be surprising to find Hinduism the dominant religion of the twenty-first century. It would be a religion that doctrinally is less clear-cut than mainstream Christianity, politically less determined than Islam, ethically less heroic than Buddhism, but it would offer something to everybody... Hinduism will spread not so much through the gurus and swamis, who attract a certain number of people looking for a new commitment and a quasi-monastic life-style, but it will spread mainly through the work of intellectuals and writers, who have found certain Hindu ideas convincing and who identify them with their personal beliefs. A fair number of leading physicists and biologists have found parallels between modern science and Hindu ideas. An increasing number of creative scientists will come from a Hindu background, will consciously, and unconsciously blend their scientific and their religious ideas. All of us may be already much more Hindu than we think."

George Ifrah (born in 1947), author of *The Universal History of Numbers*, quotes 24 passages from Indian scriptures to support the ancient knowledge of mathematics. He noticed the connection between mathematics and metaphysical abstractions, and exalts the scientific character of Sanskrit, highlighting the fact that the very term *samskrita* means precisely "perfect, complete, definitive". He wrote, "A thousand years ahead of Europeans, Indian savants knew that the zero and infinity were mutually inverse notions."

Brian David Josephson (born in Wales, 1940), pioneer of superconductivity and magnetic fields, director of the project of Unification Mind-Matter, and Nobel Prize 1973 for physics, wrote, "The Vedanta and the Sankhya hold the key to the laws of mind and thought process which are co-related to the Quantum Field, i.e. the operation and distribution of particles at atomic and molecular levels."

Another theoretical physicist, Bernard Enginger (1923-2007), had taken the vedic name of Satprem. Member of the French resistance during the World War 2, he was arrested by the Gestapo and spent 18 months in a concentration camp, then at the end of the war he went to India where he served under the colonial French government at Pondicherry, where he discovered Aurobindo and Mère.

He wrote, "Which sadist God has decreed that we would have only one life to realize ourselves and through which colossal ignorance Islam and Christianity have decided that we shall go to Heaven or Hell, according to the deeds, bad or good, which we have committed in a single life?"

Many other Westerners have openly converted to Hinduism. We may mention for example Ram Dass (born Richard Alpert in 1931) author of *Be Here Now* and disciple of Neem Karoli Baba.

Another well known personality is Satguru Sivaya Subramuniyaswami (1927-2001), American by birth, editor of the magazine *Hinduism Today*. He wrote, "Hinduism is so broad. Within it there is a place for the insane and a place for the saint...There is a place for the intelligent person and plenty of room for the fool. Hinduism, the Eternal Way or Sanatana Dharma, has no beginning, therefore will certainly have no end. It was never created, and therefore it cannot be destroyed. It is a God-centric religion. The center of it is God. All of the other religions are prophet-centric."

Daya Mata (1914-2010), president and *sanghamata* ("Mother of the Association") of Self Realization Fellowship, Los Angeles, and Yogoda Satsanga in India for 55 years. Born Faye Wright in a prominent family of the Church of Jesus Christ of Latter-day Saints, descendent of the early Mormon pioneers, wrote *Only Love': Living the Spiritual Life in a Changing World, Finding the Joy Within You: Personal Counsel for God*

Centered Living, and *Enter the Quiet Heart: Creating a Loving Relationship with God*.

Swami Kriyananda (born J. Donald Walters in 1926), disciple of Paramahamsa Yogananda (1893-1952) and minister of his church called Self Realization Fellowship, wrote more than 100 books (including *The New Path, The Essence of Self-Realization* and *Conversations with Yogananda*) and composed 400 music pieces. He speaks English, Italian, Romanian, Greek, French, Spanish, German, Hindi, Bengali and Indonesian. In 1962 he left the SRF and founded Ananda, a global movement of spiritual communities based on "simple living, high thinking", with 1000 full time residents. In 1973 he founded a schooling system called Education for Life based on an ecumenical curriculum open to students of all religions, and later he produced movies on Francis of Assisi and Jesus Christ.

In contrast, David Frawley (also known as Pandit Vamadeva Shastri, a name he received from Avadhuta Shastri), has focused on traditional hinduism, vedic astrology, yoga and Ayurveda. He was the first westerner to receive the title of Jyotish Kovid from the Indian Council of Astrological Sciences (ICAS) in 1993. Founder and director of the American Institute for Vedic Studies in Santa Fe (New Mexico), he is also professor at the Hindu University of America in Orlando (Florida). Author of *How I Became a Hindu, Arise Arjuna : Hinduism and the modern world, Awaken Bharata: A Call for India's Rebirth, Hinduism and the Clash of Civilizations, Gods, Sages, and Kings, From the River of Heaven, Hinduism: The Eternal Tradition (Sanatana Dharma), The Myth of the Aryan Invasion Theory, In Search of the Cradle of Civilization, The Rig Veda and the History of India, Yoga and Ayurveda, Tantric Yoga, Wisdom of the Ancient Seers, Yoga and the Sacred Fire, Oracle of Rama, Ayurvedic Healing, Ayurveda and Marma Therapy, Yoga for Your Type: Ayurvedic Guide to Your Asana Practice, Ayurveda: Nature's Medicine, Yoga of Herbs: Ayurvedic Guide to Herbal Medicine, Ayurveda and the Mind, Astrology of the Seers, Ayurvedic Astrology.* He speaks of the need to develop a new intelligentsia composed by intellectual *kshatriyas* ("warriors") trained in Vedic dharma to face cultural challenges. He writes, "Hinduism honors the Earth as the Divine Mother and encourages us to honor her and help her develop her creative potentials. The deities of Hinduism permeate the world of nature...they don't belong to a single country or book only... I see Hinduism as a religion eminently suited for all lands and for all people because it requires that we connect with the land and its creatures - that we align our individual self with the soul of all beings around us."

Some other great thinkers among our contemporaries who have openly taken a stand, with words and action, in support of the enormous value of vedic knowledge are also Koenraad Elst (from Holland), Michel Danino and François Gautier (from France).

Michel Danino (born in 1956) from a Jewish family emigrated from Morocco, has been living in Tamil Nadu for about 30 years. Author of *The Invasion That Never*

Was, The Indian Mind Then and Now, Arise Awake to the New Indian Age, The Lost River: On the trail of the Sarasvati, L'Inde et L'invasion de nulle part, and *Kali Yuga or The Age of Confusion*. He is also the convener of the International Forum for India's Heritage.

He wrote, "The so-called "New Age" trend of the 1960s owed as much to India as to America; a number of Western universities offer excellent courses on various aspects of Indian civilization, and if you want to attend some major symposium on Indian culture or India's ancient history, you may have to go to the U.S.A; some physicists are not shy of showing parallels between quantum mechanics and yogic science; ecologists call for a recognition of our deeper connection with Nature such as we find in the Indian view of the world; a few psychologists want to learn from Indian insights into human nature; hatha yoga has become quite popular... Western civilization, not even three centuries after the Industrial Revolution, is now running out of breath. It has no direction, no healthy foundations, no value left except selfishness and greed, nothing to fill one's heart with. India alone has preserved something of the deeper values that can make a man human, and the world will surely be turning to them in search of a remedy to its advanced malady... In fact, since the start of the Judeo-Christian tradition, the West broke away from Nature and began regarding her as so much inanimate matter to be exploited (a polite word for plunder). The contrast with the ancient Indian attitude is as stark as could be. Indian tradition regards the earth as a goddess, Bhudevi

; her consort, Vishnu, the supreme divinity, incarnates from age to age to relieve her of the burden of demonic forces... 'Heaven is my father; my mother is this vast earth, my close kin,' says the Rig-Veda (I.164.33)."

Koenraad Elst (born in 1959 in Belgium in a Flamish family), author of *The Saffron Swastika, Decolonising The Hindu Mind - Ideological Development of Hindu Revivalism* and *Negationism in India: Concealing the Record of Islam*, wrote, "The struggle of Hindu society is not primarily with the Muslim community. The most important opponents of Hindu society today are not the Islamic communal leaders, but the interiorized colonial rulers of India, the alienated English-educated and mostly Left-leaning elite that noisily advertises its 'secularism'. It is these people who impose anti-Hindu policies on Hindu society, and who keep Hinduism down and prevent it from proudly raising its head after a thousand years of oppression... The worst torment for Hindu society today is this mental slavery, this sense of inferiority which Leftist intellectuals, through their power positions in education and the media, and their direct influence on the public and political arena, keep on inflicting on the Hindu mind... Most Western scholars positively dislike Hinduism when it stands up to defend itself. They prefer museum Hinduism."

François Gautier (born in 1950), political analyst for the French daily paper *Le Figaro* and defender of Indian nationalism, author of *A Western journalist on India : The Ferengi's Columns, Rewriting Indian History* and *A New History of India*. He wrote, "Ancient Hindus were intensely secular in spirit, as their spirituality was absolutely non-sectarian - and still is today in a lesser measure. Seven thousand years ago, Vedic sages, to define the Universal Law which they had experienced within themselves on an occult and supra-spiritual plane... Hinduism is probably the only religion in the world which has never tried to convert others, or conquer other countries to propagate itself as a new religion. The same is not true of Islam and Christianity... O members of the Indian intelligentsia! You think that reading the latest New York Times bestseller, speaking polished English, and putting down your own countrymen, specially anybody who has a Hindu connection, makes you an intellectual. But in the process you have not only lost your roots, you have turned your back on a culture and civilisation that is thousands of years old and has given so much to the world... For the greatness of India is spiritual. The world has lost the truth. We have lost the Great Sense, the meaning of our evolution, the meaning of why so much suffering, why dying, why getting born... But India has kept this truth. India has preserved it through seven millennia of pitfalls, genocides, and mistakes."

The Study of Vedic Scriptures in Indian History

In the previous chapter we have seen how Vedic knowledge was systematically attacked and weakened by the invasions suffered by India in the course of centuries, and how still today such negative effects are influencing the image that Indians have of the Vedas and Hindu tradition. The most serious problem is the cultural inferiority complex in the majority of Indians in general and especially in Hindus.

An important symptom is the naive and uninformed utilization of definitions that contain a negative meaning, such as "idol", "mythology", or "legend", that usually almost all Hindus use to refer to the sacred images and stories of Hinduism, while they would never dream of applying them to the Christian or Muslim equivalents. Other definitions that communicate a distorted meaning, that demeans the original sense, are for example "seer" to indicate a *rishi* and "incantation" or "litany" to refer to a *mantra*.

Equally symptomatic is the utilization - especially by those who want to pass as "intellectuals" - of definitions of typically Christian origin to refer to Hindu concepts having very different meanings: for example "pontiff" to refer to an *acharya, mahanta* or *guru*, "monk" to refer to a *brahmachari* or *sannyasi*, "priest" for a *brahmana* or *pujaka*, and "caste" to indicate *varna* as well as *jati* and *kula*.

Actually these Sanskrit words do not have a precise translation in the western languages, because they refer to very specific concepts - just like the words *yoga, ashrama, dharma* and *karma*, that would require several lines of explanation in order to be translated adequately, and therefore are better left in their original form, so much that they have officially entered the vocabulary of other languages.

In the west, many of those who study Hinduism and Vedic culture have already adopted the original definitions - such as *guru, acharya, brahmana, sannyasi, brahmachari, pujaka, varna* etc - but strangely Indians themselves show a greater attachment for the bad English translations, that in their eyes seem to lend a kind of "respectable aura" to the Indian concepts.

Also persisting, albeit in a smaller measure, is the obsolete anglicization of the spelling of the original terms when they are written in western letters - such as *hindoo, pooja, mutt, teertha, sreeman* and so on, and the unnecessary use of English words and expressions within conversations in Hindi, even by people who practically have no knowledge of the English language, and ironically by people who are openly hostile to the use of English as "colonial" and "foreign" and who want to impose the use of Hindi over the entire Indian territory and in the contacts with foreigners or people who have a different mother-tongue... for the purpose of highlighting their dedication to the cause of Indian nationalism.

Even more significant is the frequent reference to the idea that all religions are equally valid (*sarva dharma samabhava*) and therefore a Hindu who does not claim to appreciate Bible, Gospels and Koran is watched suspiciously or even openly accused of "Hindu fundamentalism", while nobody expects Christians or Muslims to appreciate Vedic scriptures as much as their own scriptures, or even just to recognize the genuineness and legitimacy of Vedic scriptures or Hindu tradition.

This creates a paradoxical situation, in which openly and publicly insulting Vedic scriptures constitutes a legitimate exercise of freedom of religion, while defending them constitutes a crime and a proof of intolerance, if not even an act of inciting to hatred and violence. So the great majority of Hindus feel compelled to abundantly praise the Christian and Islamic scriptures, even without having any knowledge of them.

Thus Shirdi Sai Baba, Brahmo Samaj, Arya Samaj, Ramana Maharshi, Paramahamsa Yogananda, Ramakrishna, Vivekananda and many others after them have felt and still feel the need to validate their own ideological position with frequent quotes, recognition, appreciation and praise for the Christian ideology. Rare exceptions are for example Swami Dayananda Sarasvati of Arsha Vidya Gurukulam and Pejawar Visvesha Tirtha Swami.

This sense of subordination towards the abrahamic ideology, not only in India but at global level, has created the widespread idea that the most representative form of Vedic or Hindu knowledge and culture is monism, sometimes modified in a drastic manner towards impersonalism, that was more digestible for the Islamic or protestant Christian iconoclasts, who still consider "diabolic" the tradition of worshiping the visible forms of the Godhead, especially the multiple forms - an iconoclastic position that was unfortunately absorbed and carried on by the Arya Samaj.

The only "personalist" form of Hinduism that is tolerated by this colonial-type ideological tendency is Vaishnavism, especially presented as an absolute monotheism focused on a male God, usually identified as the God of the Bible and Koran. In this context, the Gaudiya Vaishnavism presents Chaitanya as the divine incarnation in the garb of a prophetic figure equated to the figure of Jesus Christ in christianity.

It is important to remember this fact when we see that the majority of the presentations on Vedic knowledge presently available to the public have been produced by colonialists of Christian faith, by "impersonalist" monists or by monotheistic Vaishnavas that have become institutionalized in a church-like form. Later on in the chapter we will see how the present Hindu Resurgence is striving to overcome these limitations, that are detrimental to the understanding of the genuine and original Vedic knowledge.

Another symptom of the Hindu cultural inferiority complex is the passive acceptance of non-verified negative concepts, such as the idea that Vedic tradition is the origin of the so-called "social evils" of India, such as the mistreatment of women, the mistreatment of "low castes" and "outcaste people" generally known as *dalit* or "downtrodden" and the opposition against scientific or cultural progress. Unfortunately, due to a widespread ignorance many Hindus have embraced these negative concepts and keep propagating and defending them as if they were genuine Vedic teachings of the so-called "ancient tradition"... although they are systematically unable to quote the appropriate passages from the original scriptures. For a very simple reason: they do not exist.

The propaganda by the Christian missionaries and the colonialist literature have painted Hinduism in dark tones, for example quoting the immolation of widows on the funeral pyre of their husbands; there is a famous story described by Jules Verne in his *Around the world in 80 days*, where the British hero Phineas Fogg saves a young Indian woman who was precisely going to be killed in that way. Such propaganda also claims that Vedic tradition is at the root of the arranged or forced marriages based on profit considerations, female infanticide, child marriages, and some kind of prostitution connected to the temples. Nothing of these is prescribed by Vedic culture - neither by the original texts nor by their commentaries or by the general ethics on which their practical application is based.

However, it is true that under the Muslim domination in India unmarried women were in a disadvantaged and difficult position, because they were more exposed to the danger of sexual exploitation by the invaders. Often the widows of the warriors that had fallen on the battlefield chose mass suicide (*jauhar*) rather than the inevitable rape, followed by the sufferings of slavery. For this same reason the warriors of a besieged fort prepared themselves for battle by wearing the saffron colored clothes of a *sannyasi*.

Vedic civilization considers the possibility tat at the death of her husband a woman may feel an overwhelming sense of loss, considering herself devoid of the support and protection she wanted, and may not wish to continue to live in that condition. In such case she could freely choose to kill herself in order to be immediately reunited to the husband's soul and follow him in his next destination, on the heavenly planets or in a new earthly incarnation. The western tradition, too, has witnessed similar sentiments. Their most famous expression is seen in Juliet and Romeo, described by the beautiful tragedy written by William Shakespeare. Such sentiments can be observed even among animals, that sometimes let themselves die when they lose their life companion. Such choice is severely condemned by the Christian ideology as a major sin deserving eternal hell, irrespective of the circumstances that prompted it; on the other hand it is considered legitimate in the Vedic ethics, that sees death as a normal fact of life, a simple passage from one incarnation to another, along a path of personal evolution. In the Vedic ideological system there is no eternal hell and nobody has the authority to judge what another person does with his or her own body. Based on these considerations, suicide (of women and men alike) is not condemned - although it is not recommended either, and certainly it is not prescribed. And certainly there is no authorization for false suicide - that is to say, homicide passed as suicide on the basis of social or cultural pressure or even committed by violence.

In Vedic culture, the fundamental factor is not death in itself - which is an inevitable and often liberating passage - but the type of awareness that a person has at the moment of death, as it is confirmed for example in *Bhagavad gita* (8.6). The entire human life is a preparatory course for the moment of death, that must be faced with the maximum respect and the maximum attention, to ensure a favorable birth in the next life.

In western countries this perspective is only recently being understood and appreciated, for example by those who oppose prolonged artificial life support for patients that are in desperate and irreversible conditions, especially when the patient himself/herself has expressed the intention of being allowed to die in a serene and dignified way.

In any case, as we have already mentioned, the choice of voluntarily leaving one's body is never suggested or prescribed by Vedic tradition, and the original texts only describes a very small number of cases. For example, there is the story of Sati, Shiva's wife, who decided to leave her body as an act of protest against the offensive behavior of her father Daksha against her because she had chosen to marry Shiva. Sati's suicide, committed by awakening the inner fire from within her body and using it to consume the body itself, was therefore a rejection of the relationship with the physical body of which Daksha could claim to be the father. Sati considered Daksha as an unworthy person, with whom she did not want to have any relationship any more.

Popular ignorance, reinforced by the distorted propaganda of colonialism, has connected this radical choice of Sati's with the idea of the widow that immolates herself (or worse, that is immolated) on the funeral pyre of her husband, precisely called *sati* - forgetting that Sati's suicide has nothing to do with widowhood. Shiva had certainly not died. On the contrary, many *Puranas* clearly describe this very famous episode and say that Shiva, informed about the death of his beloved wife, became extremely angry and rushed to the spot, taking the dead body of his wife in his arms, and immediately decided to punish the offender that had caused such a drastic gesture.

Other examples of self-immolation are described in regard to Self-realized *yogis* and *yoginis* and *tapasvis/tapasvinis* (both males and females) who left their bodily sheath exactly in the way used by Sati and in circumstances chosen in conscious and deliberate way - but never dictated by despair and fear as it is the norm with ordinary suicides. This factor gives a superior dignity and glory to such action, transcending the identification with a particular material body and offering the opportunity of liberation or a better birth.

In the light of these considerations, we can better understand the reasons why, during the late middle ages, under the Islamic threat or domination, some Hindu women chose to commit suicide at the death of their husband - also because this action discouraged those who could consider the killing of the husband of an attractive woman as an easy and convenient method to force her into their own harem, something that used to happen frequently in those times.

On the basis of similar considerations, the fathers of young girls tended to be quick in officializing the marriage of their daughters to guarantee them a better protection. According to the Islamic law, a married woman belongs to her husband (even if he is of a very low social condition) and it is more difficult to get her into the harem of another man.

We see from the descriptions of the *Puranas* that in Vedic society girls marry only after attaining the "marriageable age", when they actually desire to unite with a man and have children, directly choosing their future husband, and there is not even one single mention of a marriage in pre-pubescent age. On the other hand, still today the Islamic ideology teaches that it is perfectly moral and legitimate to organize or force marriage on a pre-pubescent girl, following for example the model offered by Mohammed himself, who at the age of 52 married Ayesha, a little girl that was only 6 years old. In the *Tahrirolvasyleh* of Ayatollah Khomeini (volume IV, published in 1990) we even find the following statement: "It is not illicit for an adult male to have a sexual relationship with a girl that is still in her weaning age".

Because according to the Muslim logic it is normal that a married woman is kept within the house under the strict control of her husband, the Hindu families that married their daughters at a very young age could keep their girls out of sight for their better protection. On the other hand, the *brahma vadinis*, *devadasis* and *ganikas*, the "independent women" that had been very respected in Vedic society, became fully exposed to the danger of sexual exploitation under the new norms imposed by the Islamic government, so their tradition totally disappeared, substituted by vulgar prostitution - often forced prostitution or sex slavery.

The legal system of *sharia*, introduced in India under the Muslim domination and only partially abolished by the British regime, imposes considerable restrictions to women's rights, including the right to property, to inheritance and to court witness. For example, according to the *sharia* a raped woman must bring at least one male witness supporting her declarations, so that her version can have more weight than the rapist's word who chooses to deny the facts. Failing which, she will be subjected to severe corporal punishment (including stoning) for the crime of adultery, as we often hear from international news. If the raped woman and her supporting witness are non-Muslims while the rapist is a Muslim, she will require no less than 4 male witnesses to support her claims. This system of legislation can still be seen in the countries with an Islamic government, as in Saudi Arabia, and in Islamic reference texts regarding women's rights, that can be consulted on many internet websites.

Many, even among Hindus, believe that the *purdah*, i.e. the segregation of women and the obligation for women to remain completely covered or at least "as covered as possible" in public, is a "morality" value characteristic of Hinduism based on "shyness". It is easy to disprove this myth, simply by visiting one of the few surviving temples among those that had been built and decorated before the Muslim invasions. The more ancient are the temples, the more we can find many depictions of women that are very scantily dressed: anyone can observe the joyful and serene exaltation of the beauty and glory of the human body as a religious value in itself. And these are not simply depictions of female dancers or ordinary women visiting the temple: they include women worshipers, painted or sculpted in the act of personally fanning the Deity or offering various worship articles - and even the female Deities themselves, whose majestic and splendid physical forms are amply revealed to the devotees. Someone may object that such Deities were sculpted with very little clothing because the worship method precisely includes the offering of clothing as dress, but even a quick verification will show that the sculpted image is already adorned not just with some clothing (although rather revealing), but even with a wealth of beautiful ornaments, including crowns, belts and necklaces. On the other hand, the images of female Deities sculpted or painted after the period of the Muslim and British dominations usually come as a sort of monolithic bloc, where the clothing completely covers and hides the body.

The technical term defining these paradigms is *laukika sraddha* or "popular belief", devoid of factual value because it is opposed to *shastra pramana*, or authoritative "scriptural foundation".

Another of these silly beliefs claims that Hindu girls or women, especially from "good families", should not receive any cultural or professional education, so that they will remain more "faithful and obedient" to their husband and in-laws, because they totally depend on them. Instead of "getting ideas" about their own personal value as individuals within the family and society, these women should simply concern themselves to produce a sufficient number of male children. This idea, that is certainly offensive towards women, has infiltrated into the mass of other prejudices cultivated by ignorant people, but does not have any foundation in the genuine vedic Tradition.

On the contrary, in the original scriptures and especially in the very little known *Kama sutra*, we read that girls, especially those from good families, including princesses, were encouraged to learn the 64 arts, thanks to which they would become able to bring prosperity to their home and even get independent income in case of widowhood or financial difficulties of the husband or his family - as the text explicitly states.

Such arts include the study of foreign languages, gastronomy and culinary arts, medicine, gardening, the preparation of preserves, drinks, perfumes, oils and medicinal extracts, tailoring, dyeing of clothes and other materials, fashioning gold and creating jewels, the ability to evaluate the price of gems and metals, chemistry and mineralogy, metallurgy and the knowledge of mining processes, the creation of flower ornaments both for the person and for home decoration, the creation of turbans and various hair-dressing styles, tattooing, the art of service to the Deity, the art of making *malas* (rosaries) and religious decorations, magical (i.e. tantric) arts, spells and magical potions, coded languages and communications, the management of cisterns for water and storage facilities, singing, dancing, performance arts, painting, sculpting and all the figurative arts, poetry and the various literary arts, training and care of pet animals, the art of toy making, martial arts and military strategy, architecture, carpentry and ebonistery, house management and accountings, gambling, psychology (especially marital counseling), sociology, as well as the various sexual arts.

The original scriptures clearly state that the women who are expert in these arts and sciences are immensely respected in society even when they live alone independently; thanks to their personal abilities they obtain a place of respect in the city assemblies, they are praised by respectable people and become able to overcome any crisis at personal or family level.

Besides these independent professional abilities, married women could normally participate in a direct way to the professional activities of their husband. A famous example is queen Kaikeyi, who normally went to battle on her own chariot in the army of the kingdom of Ayodhya; once she entered the fight to face the great warriors that had stricken king Dasaratha unconscious. After defeating and routing the generals of the enemy army, Kaikeyi picked up the unconscious body of her husband, moved him to her own chariot and took him to safety, saving his life. For this action, Dasaratha had promised to repay his debt by fulfilling any request from her.

Similarly, the wives of *brahmanas* and *vaisyas* were welcomed to directly participate to the professional activities of their families if they so desired.

The ignorant notion for which women should not be given any education, however elementary, specifically because they must not be made able to honestly make a living in an independent way, obviously leads degraded people to believe that the birth of a girl child should be considered a disgrace rather than a happy event as in the case of a male child. In the most extreme cases the disapproval of the family can turn into serious neglect towards the girl all along her childhood, if not into infanticide or foeticide when the ultrasound tests reveal that the unborn child is a female.

Such ideas do not find any support in any Vedic texts, either in a theoretical or in a practical form. Rather, the teachings of the *Vedas* lead in a completely opposite direction. There are no Vedic texts that endorse, contemplate or even mention the killing of girl children or the neglect or mistreatment of girls or women, of any age. On the contrary, according to the Vedic scriptures a woman or a *brahmana* must never be subject to physical punishment or mistreatment of any kind, even when they are factually recognized as guilty of some serious crime.

Apart from being respected as visible manifestations of the Divine Feminine, women are described as perfectly equivalent counterparts to men. The *Saunaka Samhita* of *Atharva Veda* (10.8.27) states, *tvam stri tvam pumanasi*, "you (i.e. the incarnation of *atman/ brahman*) are woman and man", and *stri pumsau brahmano jatau striyah brahma utha bhavana*, "both women and men are born from the same Brahman - women are manifestations of the Supreme Being and so are men" (*Atharva Veda Paippalada Samhita* 8.9.11). The *Mahanirvana tantra* (8.47) teaches that a girl must be raised and educated with the same opportunities that are offered to male children. In Vedic civilization there is no discrimination between sons and daughters: *Rig Veda* (8.31.8) offers the description of a happy family, blessed by Indra with sons and daughters.

It is true that Vedic scriptures do not force anyone to engage above and beyond their capacities and wishes, and therefore in Vedic civilization a woman may choose to simply dedicate herself to family, children, husband, home, and concern herself about her own physical appearance without being forced to engage in other activities, but such occupations do not constitute a limitation, an obligation or a priority duty.

According to the *Harita Dharmasutra* of the Maitrayaniya school of *Yajur Veda*, women can be classified into two types: (*dvi vidha striyah, brahmavadinyah sadyovadhvas ca, tatra brahmavadini namupanayana magnindhanam svaghre bhiksha acharyeti*).

The first type of women mentioned in this *Dharma sutra* is the category of the *brahma vadinis*, those who choose to dedicate their lives to the study, practice and teaching of Vedic knowledge and Brahman realization. These transcendental and powerful women are not required to marry and raise children, although there is no rule that forbids them to do so, even later in life. Tradition offers the examples of Visvavara, Ghosha, Sikata, Nivavari, Apala and Visvavara from the family of Atri, Angirasi Sarasvati from the family of Angirasa, Yami Vaivasvati, Sraddha, Ghosha, Surya, Indrani, Urvasi, Sarama, Juhu and Paulomi Saci, who are associated to the *mantras* of *Rig Veda*.

Another famous *brahma vadini*, Lopamudra, was famous for her deep knowledge of Sanskrit and Tamil.

The meaning of her name is "completely absorbed in the Self", and we find her in the category of the Brahmavadhini Rishi-patnis, because she became the wife of Agastya Rishi. Two *mantras* of the *Rig Veda* (1.179.1-2) are attributed to her.

It is said that some Vedic scholars named their literary work from their wives or daughters, as in the case of the *Vedanta* commentary called *Bhamati* and the mathematic treatise called *Lilavati*. However, we cannot dismiss the possibility that such texts have in fact been written or composed by the women whose names they bear, because there is no specific documentation for the authorship of these works.

The *Rig Veda suktas* 10-134, 10-39, 10-40, 10-91, 10-95, 10-107, 10-109, 10-154, 10-159, 10-189 are explicitly feminine in origin; the book 14 of *Atharva Veda* and various sections in several more books are attributed to Rishikas or "female Rishis". The *Vac sukta* (*Rig Veda* 10.125), focusing on the very revelation of the *Vedas*, is attributed to the Rishika Vagambhrina. The entire book of *Atharva Veda* concerning domestic rituals, marriage etc, is attributed to a Rishika. Many parts of the other 19 books are attributed to women, and the rituals described as specifically called *strikarmani*, ceremonies specifically celebrated by women.

The ritual texts of the *Vedas* offer a list of the Rishikas to whom the student must offer his homage during the learning of the divine texts - for example the *Ashvalayana Grhyasutra* (3.4.4) and *Shankhayana*

Grhyasutra (4.10) that list female Vedic *gurus*, such as Sulabha Maitreyi and Vadava Prathiteyi. Some Vedic texts present women as authorities on the details of the Vedic rituals; for example the *Aitareya Brahmana* 2.9 quotes the opinion of Kumari Gandharva-grihita on the ritual of Agnihotra (the daily celebration of the fire sacrifice).

Some texts are specifically destined to be recited by women - like the *mantras* of the *Madhyandina Yajurveda* (5.17, 3.44-45 etc), the *Apastambha dharmasutras* (2.2.29.11-15) and the *Srauta sutras* on the Vedic ceremonies. Also many *mantras* from the *Yajur Veda* (for example *Sukla* 5.17) are specifically meant to be recited by women. Even when men recited the other *slokas*, the presence of women was implicit: the recitation of the *Sama Veda* is intended to be accompanied by the music of the instruments played by women.

In *Kena Upanishad*, Uma Brahmavidya appears to dissipate Indra's ignorance with her teachings: apparently Adi Shankara saw this discourse as very important, because he wrote no less than two different and subsequent commentaries on this one text.

The girls called *brahma vadini* underwent the vows of *brahmacharya* and the *upanayana samskara* just like boys, beginning the performance of the Agnihotra (daily fire sacrifice) and the *veda-adhyayana* (daily study of Vedic scriptures) at a very young age, with the only difference that - due to their generally more delicate physical structures - girls were not required to observe the strict rules of austerities prescribed for males. Therefore they were allowed to to spend their *brahmacharya* period in the home of their own father or in the home of other relatives, receiving a private tuition and obtaining their *bhiksha* (ritual alms) from family members rather than from strangers. This is also confirmed in another text (now lost) quoted by other commentators/ writers with the title of *Yamadharmashastra*.

However, it is important that such provision did not constitute a limitation or obligation, or a strict rule. Still in post-Vedic times, Panini wrote that girls attend Vedic schools called *charanas* (4.1.63) and that sometimes they reside in hostels or *chhatri-sala* (6.2.86) for the purpose of their studies. According to the grammarian Katyayana (4.1.14, 6.1.92), who lived after Panini, one of such schools was very famous because of the grammar course by Apisali, an illustrious grammarian who lived before Panini. In his *Mahabhasya* (2.206) Patanjali mentions a school where female students learn the Mimamsa philosophy and makes a distinction between beginner and advanced students, respectively defined by the terms *adhyetri* and *manavika* (4.193, 2.249).

When they chose to marry, the *brahma vadinis* looked for men who were equally dedicated to the cultivation of spiritual knowledge and practice. Some famous Rishi patnis, respected and famous at least as much as their husbands, were Romasa the wife of Svanya, Anasuya the wife of Atri, Maitreyi the wife of Yajnavalkya, Arundhati the wife of Vasistha, Vasukra patni, Ghosha and so on. And just like men, these *brahma vadinis* had the opportunity to go through the other traditional *ashramas* in human life, up to the level of the order of total renunciation or *sannyasa*. It is said that Gargi attained perfect realization in the stage of *brahmacharya*, Chudala in the *grihastha ashrama*, Maitreyi in the stage of *vanaprastha*, and Sulabha yogini as a *sannyasini*. This Sulabha *bhikshuni* ("sacred mendicant") was famous for her vast and deep knowledge of the *Mahabharata*.

According to the Vedic tradition the second category of women, called *sadhya vadhu*, consists of the ordinary persons who simply aspire to be housewives and mothers. They may not be particularly learned or austere, but they are much respected nonetheless, precisely for the educational role and influence they have for their children, and for the support and care they provide to all the members of the family and the clan. Unlike the women who live under the Islamic segregation regime, ordinary married women in Vedic society are totally free to move around, and they can go out in public either alone or escorted, to participate to the various social, religious or cultural functions, or for shopping or visiting pleasant or interesting places. In this regard there are many descriptions from the scriptures and historical records. However, everyone is expected to be faithful to their duties, as duty is the basis of religion, so Vedic women who are dedicated to the family and the home must give priority to such duties even in the case financial prosperity allows them to maintain servants and maidservants: the mistress of the house must supervise all work strictly. Thanks to the pleasantness and comfort of traditional Vedic housing structures, endowed with vast orchards and kitchen gardens, water tanks, storing rooms and laboratories for the home production of various goods, the "mother of the family" did not need to leave her house in order to perfectly perform her duties. In Vedic society merchants and independent service providers (such as astrologers, palmists, physicians, artists etc) were usually going from door to door to present their merchandise and services for the convenience of customers. There are no rules that prevent women from interacting with merchants (male or female), and for this reason the women of wealthy families did not need to take the trouble to go out of their homes to run errands or to enjoy the pleasures of shopping, entertainment or popular culture.

The ordinary mother of a family, called *sadhya vadhu*, was encouraged to directly participate to all the religious rituals as Guardian of Dharma, while men are excluded from the participation to some specific domestic rituals. This position of great importance for women within the religious system in the family is symbolized by the ancient tradition of the husband who walks behind the wife around the sacred fire during the marriage ceremony. Such tradition is still alive in Orissa, together with a strong devotion to the Mother Goddess - in spite of all the efforts made by invaders to demolish it, both through laws that oppress women and through the distortion of Vedic concepts, or even with the physical destructions of the texts on the subject and the qualified teachers that supported the original and genuine version.

The *brahmanas* who were famous for their learning and experience in the study of scriptures were particularly targeted during the Islamic conquest of India: normally they were slaughtered or deprived of their distinctive symbols and forced to work in extremely dangerous, exhausting and degrading conditions. For example, they were engaged in the removal of garbage, stool and dead bodies, or personal service to the conquerors. To make a small example, within the short period of the year 1393, just one ruler among many, Sultan Sikander But-Shiken, was responsible for the disappearance of about 80 thousand *brahmanas*: the number of his victims can be calculated on the basis of the 80 kg of sacred thread that he collected by eliminating those who were wearing it. Consider that the weight of one sacred thread is approximately 1 gram. The chronicles of another Islamic sultan in India, Amir Shamasu'd-Din Iraqi, openly state that every day from 1500 to 2000 *brahmanas* were brought to his palace, where they were deprived of their sacred thread, forcibly circumcised and force-fed with cow meat. If the unfortunate victims dared to return to their old religion, they were immediately slaughtered together with their families and associates.

Unfortunately in India the texts of the Muslim chronicles are difficult to access, because their free consultation by the public is considered dangerous as it could cause "communal tension". However, it is possible to find the quotes in other countries, especially where the government is openly Islamic, where the events related by such chronicles are still proudly considered as great and glorious achievements by the religious fundamentalists.

The same type of persecution targeted the texts of Vedic scriptures. While such texts were extremely numerous originally, they were decimated or mutilated in such a way that it became impossible to effectively counteract the invaders' propaganda. Nonetheless, there is still sufficient material to help us understand the true ideological position of Vedic knowledge in relation to these problems. The *Dharma shastra* text commented by Kullukabhatta (15th century CE) is missing many texts in its later versions: these texts specifically said that the wives are in charge of the daily performance of the *agnihotra* in the house. In fact according to the traditional rule a man becomes eligible to celebrate the Vedic rituals only after marriage (*Madhaviya Shankara digvijaya* 2.14) and the *samskaras* (the ritual purification ceremonies) can be successful only if the two spouses sit together (*Aitareya Brahmana* 7.10, *Rig Veda* 8.31.5-9, *Taittiriya Brahmana* 2.2.2.6, commentary by Shabara Swami sul *Purvamimamsa sutra* 6.9.17, *Siddhanta kaumudi* on *Ashtadhyayi* 4.1.33). Tradition requires the wife to support the husband's hand every time he pours the *ahuti* (ritual oblation in the sacrificial fire) to indicate that the ritual is performed jointly. However, there is no similar prescription for women when they directly celebrate the *homa* and pour the *ahuti* - something they can do independently. In the *Mahabharata* we see Savitri and Amba performing the Agnihotra, the fire sacrifice, by themselves and on their own right. This tradition is confirmed in the *Gobhila Grihasutra* (1.3.15) and in the *Asvalayana Grihasutra* (1.9), that quotes the famous female teacher Vadava Pratiteyi (3.4.4). In *Ramayana* we see Kausalya, Sita and Tara (respectively wives of Dasaratha, Rama and Sugriva) independently performing the Agnihotra, while on the occasion of Rama performing the Asvamedha yajna in the absence of his wife Sita, he is required to install a golden statue of his wife in the *yajna* site so that the process will not be invalidated.

According to Vedic scriptures, women also possess the necessary requisites to perform the daily *sandhya* rituals. In Vedic Arya society all women wear the sacred thread (*upavita*), as *brahmacharini* (celibate students) or as married women. In Dandin's *Kadambari* (8th century CE) a lady called Mahasveta is described as decorated by a white sacred thread resplending like pure moonlight.

According to the *Harita smriti*, the second category of women (*sadyo vadhus*) having more ordinary tendencies, who have not undergone the stage of *brahmacharya* and connected rituals, received their sacred thread (in the ceremony called *upanayana*) just before marriage. In fact the *Gobhila Grihasutra* (2.1.9) states that during the marriage the bride must wear the *upavita* (sacred thread) signifying that she has undergone all the *samskaras* or prescribed purification rituals, and is therefore an *arya*, a "civilized and educated person".

Manusmriti (2.145) teaches that the mother is 1000 times more venerable than the father, and many scriptures (such as *Gautama Dharmasutra* 2.57, *Yajnavalkya Smriti* 1.33, *Mahabharata* 1.196.16) state that the mother must be considered the greatest Guru for her children, before the father and even before the *brahmana* that gives initiation.

At the celebration of the Sraddha (the ritual to honor the dead) the mother is remembered and honored before the father. Furthermore, special extra ceremonies such as the Chandana dhenu sraddha are performed for the mother (but not for the father). While an unworthy father can be excluded from the Sraddha offerings performed by the son (*Vasistha Dharmasutra* 13.47, *Gautama Dharmasutra* 20.1) the mother can never be. A son is considered as directly responsible for the atonement for his mother's bad actions after her death (*Hiranyakeshin Grihasutra* 2.4.10.7, *Shankhyayana Grihasutra* 3.13.5).

A man who enters the order of *sannyasa* receives *pranama* (ritual homage) from his own father, but offers it to his mother. According to the Vedic tradition, at the time of *diksha* or initiation (*upanayana samskara*) the student approaches his mother to beg for *bhiksha* (ritual alms) and when the student returns home after completing his studies, he bows to his mother and offers her whatever he has acquired.

Devotion to mother as everybody's first Guru also remains when all other relationships are abandoned. We know about the example of Adi Shankara, who personally performed the cremation of his deceased mother in the courtyard of her own house even after he had entered the order of *sannyasa*. Still today, the Namputiri *brahmanas* perform the cremation of their family members in the courtyard of their own homes, as a homage to Adi Shankara. Chaitanya, too, was famous for his devotion towards his mother Saci. When he entered the order of *sannyasa* he approached her offering his obeisances and asked her orders about his future residence. Mother Saci told him to reside in Jagannatha Puri and he obeyed, remaining in Puri for the rest of his life.

In many cases, glorious sons are associated to the name of their mother rather than to the name of their father - like Devakiputra Krishna (also mentioned in *Chandogya Upanisad*), Rishi Aitareya (son of Itara), Mahidasa of *Aitareya Upanishad*, Dakshiputra Panini (the grammarian) and Kaunteya Arjuna, and obviously all the main Devas, called Adityas ("sons of Aditi").

In *Taittiriya Upanisad* (1.11.2) the teachers speak to the students of Vedic knowledge, recommending them to first offer their homage to their own mother as a manifestation of the Divine. In the famous dedication song of the devotee, God is first celebrated as Mother and then as Father: *tvam eva mata ca pita tvam eva.*

A very well-known teaching recommends all men to consider all women as their mothers, as manifestations of the one Mother Goddess, she who gives life to everyone.

Manu smriti states, *yatra naryastu pujyante, ramante tatra devata*: where women are venerated the Gods are pleased, but where they are not honored, no sacred ritual can give fruits. The houses where women are not properly honored and therefore pronounce a curse, completely perish. In the marriage hymn of the *Rig Veda* (10.85.26) it is said that the bride "addresses the assembly like a general addresses the army". Then *Rig Veda* continues (10. 159.2) describing the position of a married woman in the words of Sachi Paulomi: "I am the banner. I am the guide. I possess excellent eloquence; my husband cooperates with me and follows my will."

Rig Veda (1.73.3) describes the Divine Reality as manifested in the "glorious wife of the worshiper", that is formally venerated as Griha Lakshmi, the personification of the house's prosperity (*Taittirya Brahmana* 2.9.4.7, *Manusmriti* 9.26), "auspicious" (*Rig Veda* 3.53.6), "very auspicious" (*Rig Veda* 10.85.37), "worthy of worship" (*Mahabharata* 5.38.11), that must be treasured by her husband more than his own life itself, worshiped as a mother and respected as an elder sister (*Mahabharata* 4.3.13). The husband must never do anything that displeases his wife (*Mahabharata* 1.74) because this would make all rituals ineffective.

Still today in Hinduism, the most important and popular religious festivities are dedicated to the Mother Goddess - like Navaratri (the seasonal celebration of "nine nights"), Durga puja, Divali and so on. The appearance of Sri Rama and his victory are both celebrated in the immediate vicinities of the Navaratri festival, because it is said that Rama was able to defeat Ravana and to return to Ayodhya to be crowned there as king, only by the grace of Mother Durga, who was devoutedly worshiped by Rama.

Before participating to the battle of Kurukshetra, Arjuna worshiped Mother Durga, following Krishna's instructions.

The famous *Devi mahatmya* in the *Markandeya Purana* describes how the Mother Goddess, on the request of all the Devas and for the purpose of protecting them, killed the demoniac Madhu and Kaitabha, Sumbha and Nishumbha, Raktabija and Dhumralochana, and Mahisha asura with all his army.

In fact the worship of the female form of the Divine seems to have been the main tradition in the ancient times, followed by a subsequent development of iconography towards the masculine form especially after the beginning of Kali yuga, although the worship of the male Deities is done together with the Shakti or even openly subordinated to the Shakti, like in the examples of Shiva/Kali and Krishna/Radha.

Mother Kali ("the Black", identified with Time and Change) is often depicted standing over the body of

Shiva, who lies on the ground in a submissive and passive position. In the Krishna lila, beautifully represented by the great poet Jayadeva, Govinda embraces Radha's feet and worships them with love - the echo of such devotion is also found in the personal relationship of the poet with his own wife Padmavati.

Even when the female form in the Divine couple is depicted as submissive and devoted towards the Lord, the name of the Shakti is always mentioned before the name of the Lord - Sita Rama, Radhe Shyam, Uma Mahesha, Lakshmi Narayana, Sri Vishnu, etc.

Lakshmi is considered inseparable from Vishnu, as stated in the *Vishnu Purana* (1.8.17-20), where Parasara says: "Constant companion of Vishnu and Mother of the Universe, Lakshmi Devi is eternal. She is speech where Vishnu is the object of description. Where Vishnu is the law, she is policy. Where Vishnu is knowledge, she is intelligence. Where Vishnu is creator, she is creation. He is mountain, she is earth. He is pleasure, she is perfect satisfaction. Vishnu is desire, she is the object of desire. He is *yajna* (the sacrificial ritual), she is *dakshina* (the gift offered in sacrifice)."

The female forms of Sri Vidya and Gayatri are considered the personifications of knowledge, respectively in *Tantras* and *Vedas*. *Atharva Veda* (19.71.1) and many other texts state that Gayatri is "the Mother of all *Vedas*" (*namaste surya sankaro surya gayatrike amle, brahmavidye mahavidye vedamata namo 'stu te*).

No scholar or student could even imagine starting any study without first offering his homage to Goddess Sarasvati, and the annual festival of Sarasvati puja is still considered fundamental in all Indian schools. Sarasvati is often called Vag Devi ("the Goddess of Word"), mistress and teacher of all knowledge, both spiritual and material. Traditionally, the recitation of Vedic texts begins with an invocation to the Devi - *om shanno devirbhishtiye apo bhavantu* (*Atharva veda*). Specifically, this *mantra* constitutes the beginning of Pippalada's version of the *Atharva Veda*. It appears again as *mantra* 1.6.1 in Shaunaka's version of *Atharva Veda,* and in many texts even this version starts with the invocation to the Devi.

Bhumi puja, the ritual homage to Mother Earth as the *asana* of the worshiper, is an integral part of all traditional ritual ceremonies. *Rig Veda* contains various hymns dedicated to Mother Earth, and *Atharva Veda* (12.1.63) contains this beautiful hymn: "O Earth, Mother! Safely establish me in spiritual and material happiness, and in full accordance with the Heaven. O greatest of Sages! Support me in grace and splendor!"

Cereal grains, too, are considered sacred as a form of Devi Annapurna, and water is considered sacred as the form of the Goddess (*jala rupena samsthita*), that should be present in all celebrations in the form of the sacred *kalasha* or water pot, that traditionally "forms the body" of all the invoked Deities (males and females). The *kalasha* is also present over the temple domes and as an auspicious image painted inside temples and homes, especially on the occasion of festivals and certainly for marriages.

Both male and female Deities are praised in the *Apri suktas* and in the family prayers of all the 10 Rishi lineages. The primeval Goddess, Aditi or Adi Shakti, the mother of all the Devas, has a central place in these songs. Among the ancient Vedic Deities we find two Adityas ("children of Aditi") are in female form (Dhatri and Savitri). Also female are the names of the Deities called Ila, Usha, Yami, Ratri, Prithivi, Kamadhenu, Aranyani, Urvasi, and so on. All these Goddesses are mentioned as venerable in themselves, without any association with a male Deity counterpart; others - such as Saci and Rati - are mentioned together with a male companion, such as Indra and Kama respectively.

Regarding the supposed oppression of the "low castes" or "outcaste" and the rigid hereditary immobility of social position, it will suffice to read the original text of *Puranas* and *Itihasas*, for example, to find out a very different reality.

To begin with, in the original texts there is no reference to persons or categories called *dalit* ("oppressed") or *paria* ("emarginated") or "outcaste" or "untouchables" that are part of the hindu society. In fact, Vedic scriptures state that human kind (*manusya jati*) can be divided into two vast categories - *arya* and *anarya*, respectively those who follow the Vedic rules of civilized life, and those who don't. Both these definitions can be applied at individual and collective level.

These rules are based on hygienic, ethical, social and cultural principles. The most important example is cleanliness or purity: an *arya* must take a bath every day, 1 to 3 times a day according to the circumstances. After bathing in clean water, preferably running water, one must wear fresh clean clothes. In any case it is necessary to take a complete bath and wear fresh clothes in order to purify oneself from excretions - for example after going to the toilet or in case of vomit, sexual secretions, mucus secretions, bleeding etc. The general rule becomes even stricter when the individual is engaged in activities that require a higher hygienic level, such as food preparation, water management (especially drinking water) and all those religious activities with a public distribution of food, water, flowers, leaves and other substances that have been offered to the Deity and that are traditionally eaten or drunk with great respect by people.

The need of cleanliness and purity also applies to one's food habits through vegetarianism as the abstention from substances that are intrinsically impure such as the bodies of dead animals, as well from substances that can contaminate the mind such as alcoholic drinks or some plants containing active principles with undesirable effects.

The second fundamental principle of Vedic civilization is the individual's evolution of awareness through study and personal discipline, the participation to social prosperity through the performance of professional duties (irrespective of the profit that one can get), the responsibility towards one's family and ancestors, gratitude and respect towards one's superiors, gradual detachment from temporary identifications and material attachments, and liberation from all conditionings in preparation for death. These qualities are cultivated through the system of the *ashramas* or progressive stages in the life of an individual, where one is trained in one's personal evolution. In the west, the word *ashrama* is generally known for its meaning of "residence of persons who are engaged in spiritual life", but the original sense also include the meaning of "position in life".

In the first stage of life, in the *ashrama* called *brahmacharya*, the student learns to follow the rules of purity and cleanliness, studies the scriptures and applies their teachings in practice, developing a strong basis of loyalty to *dharma*, the universal rules of ethics and civilized life. In the second stage, called *grihastha*, the individual engages in economic development and prosperity by working for the family and for society without any sense of selfishness. The *grihastha* ("one who lives in his own home") faithfully performs his sacred duties, thus repaying his debt towards his ancestors, society in general and the Devas.

Gradual detachment is attained in the stage of *vanaprastha* ("that lives in the forest") when one leaves his house to his adult children and retires from social activities to devote himself to pilgrimages and austerities, until he arrives at the level of complete renunciation, called *sannyasa*, where a man abandons all fixed residence, personal property, social position and all kinds of material identifications.

Vedic or *arya* society, composed by individuals that accept to follow these rules of personal purification, is divided into four *varnas* or occupational categories, constituted respectively by *brahmanas* (intellectuals), *kshatriyas* (administrators and warriors), *vaisyas* (entrepreneurs and traders of all types) and *sudras* (craftsmen and laborers). These categories constitute the natural divisions of all human societies because they are based on spontaneous talents and tendencies that are found everywhere; the difference in Vedic society is that the *varna* system is regulated by the precise description of the qualities, the activities, the duties and the rights characteristic of each position.

Classification in one of such categories does not simply depend on birth, although birth may help considerably - just like someone who was born in a family of medical doctors or lawyers can take advantage of a favorable environment, of the constant example and of the expert guidance of his relatives. When the Vedic system and rules are strictly followed (especially in regard to the circumstances of conception) and the level of consciousness of the family is solid and consistent with the position it occupies in society, there are good probabilities that the souls attracted to take birth in that family will be positively attuned to the family traditions. In order to reinforce the positive and virtuous tendencies of the children, the parents also must perform a series of purificatory rituals that are meant to constantly elevate the level of consciousness; the number of such purification rituals (called *samskaras*) can sum up to 40, for those who choose to perform the less important ceremonies as well. Of course it is always possible to fall into accidents on the way, and sometimes it is evident that a soul who has taken birth in a particular family does not possess the necessary qualities that are required to properly carry on the family tradition. In this case the child must be offered choices that are more suitable to his actual potential.

It is also possible that in some cases affection and attachment could obscure the judgment of parents and relatives on the factual potential of a child. To counteract this danger, in Vedic society all children are sent to the Gurukula, "the family of the Guru", in the home of a qualified teacher, where they will be watched and trained in a personalized way for a certain number of years.

Since the children (generally from the age of 5 onwards) live in close contact with the Guru and his family, day and night, the teacher can easily observe their behavior in a variety of situations and evaluate which professional and social occupation each child will best perform in the future. Of course the Guru must be qualified for such task, because by his endorsement and guidance he becomes totally responsible for the success or failure of each student. Apart from the fundamental education and training on ethical and religious principles that is given to everyone, each boy is specifically engaged in one of the four occupational fields that is most suitable according to his natural tendencies and capabilities. Those who love to study and learn quickly, and show the most exemplary ethical behavior are trained as *brahmanas*, or teachers and consultants. Those who are good in organizing things (because they are able to manage people) and love physical activities are trained as *kshatriyas*, while those who have entrepreneurial tendencies (organizing materials and resources) are trained as *vaisyas*. These three categories of students receive the religious initiation or *diksha*, by which they become officially recognized as "twice born", something that includes precise duties for the performance of rituals and work for society, The less enthusiastic students, who are lazy, hungry for sense gratification, rather selfish and devoid of specific talents, unable to actually take responsibilities, remain in the generic position of *sudras* and they are simply expected to perform the duty to assist the other social categories. In exchange, their employers take care of them and their families in all aspects of life.

It is important to understand that the *sudras* are not "untouchables", *parias* or *dalits*. The life conditions of a *sudra* depend solely on his relationship with his employer and has nothing to do with social conventions or prejudice. *Sudras* are considered *aryas* and their employers treat them like their own children or family members. Because generally the *sudras* or servants live in their employer's house, the British colonialists that observed Indian society from the outside, through the lenses of their own social prejudice, mistakenly confused the position of the *sudra* with the position of the slaves in some ancient European societies. This misunderstanding has been solidified by the notorious Aryan Invasion Theory, on which we will discuss later on.

The key to correctly understand the position of the *sudra* in Vedic society consists in the analysis of the two apparently similar definitions of *dasa* ("servant") and *dasyu* ("thief, criminal"). As we have already examined, Vedic scriptures encourage each individual to evolve and improve himself. However, it may happen that some people choose to indulge in the lowest and most degrading tendencies, and tend to pick up bad habits instead of developing good habits. For example, a *sudra* can become lazy to the point of neglecting the basic hygienic and cleanliness norms, or greedy to the point of misappropriating valuable objects without the permission of the legitimate owner. Or he can become selfish to the point of showing a cruel and insensitive behavior towards people or towards animals. These violations to the rules are not extremely serious in themselves, but they create a danger for the proper functioning of society, therefore one who chooses to continue into that direction is dismissed from service and expelled from Vedic social life, thus becoming known as an *anarya* or *chandala*, a "non-civilized person". It is important to understand that the classification into the category of *anarya* or *chandala* is based on the individual's free choice of not following the basic rules of cleanliness, austerity and compassion. In the original system, this is not about birth right, and nobody is forced in that direction.

Of course we must consider the importance of the environmental factor of family in the development of a system of values for the individual - because taking birth in a degraded family exposes one to the bad example and to the bad teachings of his parents and relatives. However, this is not a decisive factor, because as we all know there are often exceptions both in the good and in the bad.

Such exceptions must be recognized and officialized by the leaders of society, specifically by the teachers (*brahmanas*) and rulers (*kshatriyas*), who have always had the power to officially modify the social position of an individual on the basis of his actual qualities, his level of consciousness and his behavior.

Apart from these exceptions, that we will examine later on, we need to understand that in general the *anaryas* (also called *chandala* or *mleccha*) constitute a cause of disturbance and danger for Vedic society, and for this reason they are not permitted to normally reside within the urban areas where civilized people live. However, they are left free to choose a fixed or nomadic residence of their liking in any area that is distant enough from urban habitation.

This effectively contradicts the picture of slavery and mistreatment that is presented by the anti-Vedic propaganda, because normally such drastic segregation does not allow sufficient conditions of contact and vicinity between members of the civilized society and members of the wild or tribal societies. In the case where a member of the civilized society (*arya*) comes in contact with a member of a non-civilized society (*anarya*), the *arya* has the duty to always behave in a kind and respectful way, because each human being deserves a basic level of respect simply because of the potential development afforded by his body. No mistreatment or coercion is ever allowed.

Svetasvatara Upanishad (II. 5) says that all human beings, without any distinction, are *amritasya putra*, "children of the Immortality", as they are heirs to spiritual realization.

Both the *Rig Veda* (5-60-5) and *Yajur Veda* (16.15) state that all human beings are members of the same family, and they are all entitled to equality. *Atharva Veda* (3-30-1) states that all human beings must have for each other the same affection and love shown by a cow to her newborn calf, they should share food and be firmly united like the spokes in a chariot wheel.

Tolerance of lifestyles that are different from ours should be based on such considerations, but it should not fall into the opposite exaggeration, by which one must give the same value to all behaviors, or even give more facilities and rights to those people who are less qualified. This would inevitably cause people to behave in the worst possible way and to avoid all effort to improve and evolve personally.

Therefore, the clear perception of the basic equality of all human beings does not invalidate the need to regulate the normal community life, because the free choices of one individual or one group of individuals should not damage other individuals or other groups of individuals.

The rules that forbid *chandalas* or *anaryas* to live in close contact with *aryas* are not based on racism or social prejudice, but simply by strictly hygienic considerations. Even when we talk of segregation, it is important to understand that it is not based on birth considerations or prejudice, and above all it is not a permanent or coercitive system, and it is not caused by a condition of financial poverty. In Vedic civilization the lack of financial resources never constitutes a reason for segregation or social discrimination, and certainly it is not the cause of impurity or contamination. Anyone can maintain his legitimate position of civilized person in Vedic society by simply accepting to keep himself decently clean, something that can be done even by regularly bathing and washing one's clothes in a river or pond, without spending any money, and abstaining from dirty and unhygienic life habits. Not even travelling beggars are assimilated to the *chandalas* - of course provided they observe the fundamental rules of hygiene and civilized behavior.

In some cases, *chandalas* can enter the urban areas if they wish to do so in order to perform some legitimate activity - for example to remove the dead bodies of human beings that are carried to the crematorium outside the city, or the bodies of animals who died of natural causes, that the *chandalas* will be allowed to utilize to get leather and meat, because they are characteristically non-vegetarian. In fact, one of the most frequent definitions for a *chandala* is *sva-pacha*, "one who cooks/ eats dog meat". The habit to consume impure foods, such as meat, fish and eggs - that are not part of the diet of *aryas* or civilized persons - constitutes an extremely important factor in the definition of *anarya* and in the necessity for them to reside in separate settlements at a distance from the *aryas*. This is not simply for the comfort of the *aryas*. For those who are attached to the consumption of non-vegetarian foods it is not convenient to live in civilized urban areas, because in such areas it is not possible to slaughter animals. In fact the *kshatriya* has the duty to protect all the *prajas*, those who have taken birth in his area - and this also includes innocent animals, those animals that do not cause damage or even constitute an asset for civilized society, as for example the cows. Characteristically, the *anaryas* do not care for such considerations and eat any animal they want to kill, therefore they prefer to live in their own villages, in the forests and on the hills, or at the delta of rivers or along the sea, where the environmental situation offers ample opportunities for hunting and fishing, and where they are free to behave according to their chosen lifestyle, even if it is disgusting, cruel and unhygienic.

When they enter civilized areas, the *chandalas* are always treated kindly, respectfully and generously, provided they abstain from behaviors that create a danger for the hygiene of the civilized community - as for example contaminating water tanks or cooked foods, or imposing unwanted and unpleasant physical contact to the inhabitants of the city. Such prohibitions are purely functional to the purpose of maintaining a rigorous public hygiene, and are comparable to the laws of contemporary societies that regulate the sanitary requirements and the behavior of those who handle food destined to the public, for example, or to the rules that require swimmers to use the bathroom and take a shower before entering into a public swimming pool.

Contemporary societies also condemn unwanted physical contacts by dirty and smelly persons, or persons who may be carriers of contagious diseases, and although usually there are no specific laws that punish the violators, nobody will be scandalized when such individuals are removed from public and private places by security guards. In this regard it is important to notice that among the characteristics defining the *chandala* category there is the uncontrolled consumption of alcoholic beverages and other intoxicating substances that distort the state of awareness and the perception of reality - something that in contemporary western societies is often considered a crime proper.

When they perform a service of transportation of dead bodies to the crematorium, the *chandalas* always receive gifts or payment from the relatives of the deceased, and they are allowed to keep the valuable ornaments that remain among the ashes after cremation. Often a small number of *chandalas* choose such occupational profession in a permanent way and establish their residence within a crematorium or in its immediate vicinity, obtaining further income from the collection and selling of firewood for the cremation. Often the members of this particular category of "undertakers" are financially very prosperous and can afford servants and luxuries of various kinds, as we can still see today, for example among those who work in the cremation *ghats* in Varanasi (Benares). This is not a recent development, because in the puranic story of emperor Harischandra we find that the king fell from his position and ended up as the servant of a *chandala* who worked in a crematorium.

Another traditional occupational position for a *chandala* consists in the removal and treatment of garbage in general, or the cleaning and maintenance of sewage. Although Vedic civilization produces a very small amount of garbage if compared to the consumeristic industrial culture based on plastic and "disposable" products and packaging, there is always a certain amount of detritus that will be found in an urban area - for example broken utensils and containers, worn out and damaged clothes or furniture and so on. All these discarded materials must be taken out of the city to a suitable place, and they are generally recycled, which creates another occupational opportunity for those who do not have particular abilities or talents, and are not very concerned about hygienic rules.

It is important to understand that Vedic society does not need *chandalas* to perform these services, because there is no rule that prohibits the four social categories (*sudras, vaisyas, kshatriyas* and *brahmanas*) to personally perform even the "dirtiest" jobs for themselves. In other words, anyone can perform any work within one's own house or family, including the ordinary and extraordinary activities of cleanliness and the removal of dead bodies.

Besides, the *sudras* who works as servants and assistants to the other three occupational categories normally perform such services for the family of their employers, but they are not considered as *chandalas*, for the simple reason that they normally observe the rules of cleanliness and hygiene. Many people confuse the category of *sudras* with the category of *chandalas*, but these are very different positions: as we have already mentioned, the *sudras* live in the same house with the family that employs them and are considered family members.

The contamination associated with the occasional performance of impure or dirty activities, such as the transportation and cremation of dead bodies and the cleaning of animal detritus, the removal of garbage and the cleaning of sewage systems is a temporary problem and can easily be removed with a nice full bath, a change of clothes and in the case of the three social categories of "twice born", they simply need to change their sacred thread with a new clean one. Also, there are some simple ceremonies of ritual purification, especially for those who are engaged in delicate tasks, such as the worship of Deities and the preparation of food that will be distributed as *prasada*.

Furthermore, all social categories, including the highest, go through a period of ritual contamination on the occasion of a death or birth in their family; for 10 days the concerned persons cannot perform the usual rituals, visit temples or sacred places, or touch sacred objects, because they consider themselves temporarily impure. At the end of the prescribed period such contamination is removed by the physical and ritual purification that we have mentioned.

The persons who live as *chandalas* outside the Vedic rules of purification can also enter the urban areas inhabited by the *aryas* to sell useful products that they had collected outside the city - for example conchshells and pearls, ivory, wood and firewood, feathers from peacocks and other birds, hides and leather, wild honey, medicinal herbs and other forest products, as well as gardening soil, clay and so on. Such merchandises are considered pure (for example honey is a natural antibiotic) or they can easily be purified before being used.

When the *chandalas* or *mlecchas* consider their impure life habits as a valid ethnic and cultural tradition, they take a tribal name according to the particular ethnic or cultural group to which they belong: the *nishadas* are the members of wild tribes that live by hunting in the forests or deserts (with a life style that is typical for example of some african tribes), the *pulindas* are the peoples belonging to the patriarchal Greek culture, the *yavanas* are the peoples who lived in the arabian region (considered the descendants of Maharaja Yayati), the *kiratas* and *khasas* are peoples of mongolian culture, the *hunas* are the Huns, and so on. In this case, too, the condition of "uncivilized" people is conditioned to the choice of not observing the rules of hygiene and civilized life, and become obsolete when an individual agrees to follow the civilized rules, and even more so when he engages in personal evolution towards a level of transcendental consciousness.

Bhagavata purana (2.14.18) unambiguously declares: *kirata hunandhra pulinda pulkasa abhira sumbha yavanas khasadaya, ye 'nye ca papa yad apasrasrayah sudhyanti tasmai prabhavisnave namah,* "Kiratas, Hunas, Andhras, Pulindas, Pulkasas, Abhiras, Sumbhas, Yavanas, Khasas and others (similar groups), even those who were born in still more degraded cultures, are immediately purified when they put themselves under the guidance and protection of those who have taken shelter in Vishnu. Therefore I offer my homage to the all-powerful Sri Vishnu."

Even the historical chronicles and archaeological findings confirm that often individuals or entire populations of foreign origin chose to become part of Vedic society, adopting Sanskrit names and the rules of the *varna ashrama*, like for example the Scythian kings who became known as Satyasimha and Rudrasena.

Because Vedic society does not force anyone to perform specific actions or to follow rules, the *anaryas* and *chandalas* are even free to choose to become robbers. This was the case of the family of origin of Valmiki Rishi, the famous author of the *Ramayana*, who after meeting Narada Rishi renounced his uncivilized way of life and became a great *brahmana*.

In fact, at any time, any member of the various categories of *anaryas* can decide to purify himself and reform his habits, under the guidance of *arya brahmanas*, and become a part of the civilized community, in the very least in the position of *sudra* or generic laborer. From that position, he will be allowed to evolve further. In the exceptional case of a person who was born in a family of *anaryas* but already naturally possesses the level of consciousness of an *arya* or even of a *brahmana*, his actual position must be immediately recognized without the need of intermediate passages.

The greatest *brahmana*, Veda Vyasa, who compiled the entire *corpus* of Vedic literature, was the son of a woman from the fishermen community (considered in the category of *chandalas*).

His mother Satyavati was engaged in ferrying the travelers by boat on the river Yamuna, and this is how she met Parasara Rishi; the boat girl was very attracted by the Rishi, but she was ashamed of the fish stench emanating from her own body; when the Rishi realized that, he was moved and by a special blessing he transformed the stench into a very sweet scent, then the couple retired to a small island on the river. These were the circumstances of the birth of Vyasadeva, also called Dvaipayana Vyasa precisely because he was conceived on an island (*dvipa*). Parasara immediately resumed his traveling without marrying the girl, and later on Satyavati became the wife of king Santanu, from whom she had more children, as described in the *Mahabharata*.

The *Rig Veda* (9.63.5) clearly states that all human beings must make an effort to become civilized: *krnvanto visvam aryam* - "everyone should become *aryas*".

The colonialist myth according to which belonging to the class of *aryas* is determined by the genes of the "aryan race" will be amply refuted later on, when we will speak about the famous theory of aryan invasion in India. Here we will simply quote some traditional scriptures to demonstrate that anyone can become an *arya*, provided he accepts to follow the rules of civilized life in his own life. According to the original scriptures, the fundamental rule of civilized life consists in personal evolution, purification and cultivation of Vedic knowledge, that lead one to realize the Self at the spiritual and religious level.

The *Bhagavata Purana* (6.16.43) states: *na vyabhicarati taveksa hy abhihito bhagavato dharmah, sthira-cara-sattva-kadambesv yam upasate tv aryah*, "Aryas are those who do not hesitate to follow the Dharma prescribed by God, and who have no prejudice towards the various types of living beings."

The religious nature of the position of *arya*, identifying it with the original Hinduism, is highlighted by many passages of the scriptures and practical examples in the lives of great personalities. Again the *Bhagavata purana* (3.33.7) states: *aho bata sva-paco 'to gariyan yaj-jihvagre vartate nama tubhyam, tepus tapas te juhuvuh sasnur arya brahmanucur nama grnanti ye te,* "It is wonderful to see how those who have accepted to invoke your holy name (the prayer is addressed to Vishnu) are immediately glorified as civilized persons (*aryas*) and are called *brahmanas*, even if there were born in uncivilized families. The very fact that they call your name qualifies them for the performance of sacrifices and austerities according to tradition."

A very famous verse of *Garuda purana*, regularly used in all the daily rituals of purification and sacrifice, recites: *om apavitrah pavitro va sarvavasthan gato 'pi va yah smaret pundarikaksam sa bahyabhyantarah sucih*, "Anyone who remembers the lotus-eyed Lord (Vishnu) is immediately and completely purified, both internally and externally, irrespectively of the conditions he has gone through." The *Mahabharata* (5.88.52) states: *vrittena hi bhavaty aryo na dhanena na vidyaya*, "The requisite by which a person becomes *arya* is the level of consciousness, not scholarship or wealth."

Later on in *Bhagavata purana* (11.14.21) we find another relevant verse, spoken by Krishna: *bhaktyaham ekaya grahyah sraddhayatma priyah satam, bhaktih punati man-nistha sva-pakan api sambhavat,* "Only devotion enables one to attain me. The devotees who serve me with faith and transcendental attachment are completely purified through their devotion, even if they had been born in uncivilized families (of dog-eaters)."

It is important to note that all categories of uncivilized people are free to practice any form of worship or religiosity they prefer, including the typically brahminical cult offered to Vishnu, Shiva and the Mother Goddess - and in such case they should be considered "Hindu". Both scriptures and oral tradition present many illustrious examples, starting from Visvavasu, the tribal chief of the Sabaras or Saoras of Orissa, who lived in the forest where he worshiped the beautiful Deity of Nila Madhava, a particular form of Vishnu that later on manifested as Jagannatha. Still today the *daitas*, the most intimate servants of the Jagannatha Deity in the original temple in Puri, who have the privilege of physical contact with the Deity especially during the festivals, are Visvavasu. The entire region of Orissa (presently called Odisha) was originally populated by uncivilized tribal groups, of which many continue to exist in considerable numbers. These populations started to follow the Vedic rules after the arrival of some groups of *sasana brahmanas* invited into the region by Hindu kings for the purpose of teaching Vedic knowledge to the natives. The members of these aryanized tribal populations are generally called *vratyas*, because their purification and their vow (*vrata*) to follow the ethical rules was officialized in the particular ritual of sacrifice called *vratyastoma*.

The same concept of purification and evolution applies to the requirements for membership in one of the four *varnas* or social categories that constitute the Vedic society of the *aryas*.

Among the various popular beliefs (*laukika sraddha*) that do not have a genuine basis, there is a rather widespread misconception saying that the knowledge of Vedic scriptures is exclusive monopoly of a "caste of brahmins" to which one can belong only by birth: this creates the double disaster by which one who was not born in a family of brahmins is not allowed to study the scriptures because he does not possess the "intellectual and religious DNA" that is needed to learn their knowledge and become purified by it, while one who was born in a family of brahmins has no need to study the scriptures because his "intellectual and religious DNA" automatically makes him learned, pure and qualified by nature. Thus ignorance triumphs, because for one reason or another, nobody studies or practices.

Of course one who has even a minimum genuine knowledge of biology and psychology knows that the genetic code has nothing to do with the habits of physical and mental cleanliness, or with knowledge, wisdom, morality, honesty, truthfulness, benevolence for other living beings, generosity and professional talents. These qualities are determined partially by the environment and training, and partially by the individual tendencies that the soul carries along lifetime after lifetime, according to its particular evolutionary journey. As we have seen, each human being (whose genetic code is not seriously damaged) possesses the potential of personal evolution that can take him/her to Self realization and to the development of adequate professional and social qualities, in a more or less brilliant way. The scriptures clearly state that the system of professional and social categories is not based on birth (*jati*) but on natural talents (*guna*) and the duties actually performed (*karma*) by each individual. The Vedic scriptures quote this universally recognized and very clear statment by Atri Rishi: *janmana jayate sudra, samskarad bhaved dvijah, veda-pathad bhaved viprah, brahma janati iti brahmanah*, "By birth everybody is simply a *sudra*, while through ritual purification one becomes a twice-born, through the study of Vedic knowledge one becomes learned, and *brahmana* is one who knows Brahman."

According to *Bhagavad gita* (18.42), a *brahmana* is recognized by the following characteristics: *samo damas tapah saucam ksantir arjavam eva ca, jnanam vijnanam astikyam brahma-karma svabhava-jam*, "Peacefulness, self-control, austerity, purity, tolerance, honesty, knowledge, wisdom and religiousness - these are the natural qualities determining the duties of the *brahmana*."

The *Mahabharata* confirms: *dharmas ca satyam ca damas tapas ca amatsaryam hris titiksanasuya, yajnas ca danam ca dhrtih srutam ca vratani vai dvadasa brahmanasya*, "(A *brahmana*) must always behave in accordance to *dharma* (the ethical principles that constitute the foundations of religion). First of all he must be truthful and able to control his own senses. He must be austere, detached, humble and tolerant. He must not envy anyone. He must be expert in the performance of sacrifices and distribute his possessions in charity. He must be determined in the study of Vedic scriptures and in religious activities: these are the 12 fundamental qualities of a *brahmana*."

Again in the *Mahabharata* (Vana Parva chapter 180) we find: *satyam danam ksama-silam anrsyamsam tapo ghrna, drsyante yatra nagendra sa brahmana iti smrtah*, "A persons who is truthful, charitable, forgiving, sober, kind, austere and free from hatred is called *brahmana*."

In the *Bhagavata purana* (7.11.21) Narada Muni states: *samo damas tapah saucam santosah ksantir arjavam, jnanam dayacyutatmatvam satyam ca brahma-laksanam*, "The qualities that characterize a *brahmana* are the control of one's mind and senses, austerity and tolerance in the face of difficulties, cleanliness, contentment, tendency to forgive, simplicity, knowledge, compassion, truthfulness, and complete surrender to the Supreme Personality of Godhead."

One who does not show such qualities cannot really be considered a *brahmana*. In the *Mahabharata* (Vana Parva chapter 180), Maharaja Yudhisthira states: *sudre tu yad bhavel-laksma dvije tac ca na vidyate, na vai sudro bhavec chudro brahmano na ca brahmanah*, "If these qualities (listed as the characteristics of the *brahmanas*) are found in a *sudra* (i.e. a person born in a *sudra* family), such person must never be called a *sudra*, just like a *brahmana* (i.e. a person born in a *brahmana* family) is not a *brahmana* if he lacks these qualities."

Again the *Mahabharata* gives further clarifications in this regard (Anusasana Parva 163.8, 26, 46), where Shiva tells Parvati: *sthito brahmana-dharmena brahmanyam upajivati, ksatriyo vatha vaisyo va brahma-bhuyah sa gacchati, ebhis tu karmabhir devi subhair acaritais tatha, sudro brahmanatam yati vaisyah ksatriyatam vrajet, etaih karma-phalair devi suddhatma vijitendriyah, sudro'pi dvija-vat sevya iti brahmabravit svayam, sarvo'yam brahmano loke vrttena tu vidhiyate, vrtte sthitas tu sudro'pi brahmanatvam niyacchati.* Here is the translation: "If *kshatriyas* or *vaisyas* (i.e. persons born in *kshatriyas* or *vaisyas*) behave like *brahmanas* and engage in the occupations of *brahmanas*, such persons attain the position of *brahmana*. In the same way, a *sudra* (i.e. a person born in a *sudra* family) can become a *brahmana* and a *vaisya* can become a *kshatriya*. O Devi, thanks to the performance of these activities and by following the instructions of the *Agamas* (Vedic scriptures that contain the instructions for the rituals) even a person born in a family of *sudras* devoid of qualifications can become a *brahmana*. In this world, a person is born in a *brahmana* family as a result of his tendencies, therefore a *sudra* that manifests the tendencies of a *brahmana* and acts as a *brahmana*, automatically becomes a *brahmana*."

Another verse of the *Mahabharata* (Anusasana Parva 143.50) explains even more precisely: *na yonir napi samskaro na srutam na ca santatih, karanani dvijatvasya vrttam eva tu karanam*, "Neither birth, nor purification rituals, scholarship of ancestry constitute legitimate qualifications for the position of *brahmana*. Only the behavior as *brahmana* constitutes the basis for the position of *brahmana*."

Bhagavata purana (7.11.35) confirms: *yasya yal laksanam proktam pumso varnabhivyanjakam, yad anyatrapi drsyeta tat tenaiva vinirdiset*, "One who shows the characteristics of a *brahmana, kshatriya, vaisya* or *sudra* as described above, should be classified in the corresponding social category."

Actually, one who refuses to recognize such qualifications based on *guna* and *karma*, and rather maintains a birth prejudice and the identification with the gross body is behaving in an offensive and degrading way that automatically disqualifies him from the position of *arya*. The *Bhagavata purana* (10.84.13) states: *yasyatma buddhih kunape tri-dhatuke sva-dhih kalatradisu bhauma ijya-dhih, yat tirtha buddhih salile na karhicij janesv abhijnesu sa eva go-kharah*, "Those persons who identify the self as the gross material body, who maintain a sense of belonging to their family, who worship their native land, and who visit the sacred places simply to take a bath, are not better than animals like cows and donkeys, even if they were born as human beings."

The *Padma Purana* states: *arcye visnau sila-dhir gurusu nara-matir vaisnave jati-buddhir, visnor va vaisnavanam kali-mala-mathane pada-tirthe 'mbu-buddhih, sri visnor namni mantre sakala-kalusa-he sabda samanya buddhir, visnau sarvesvarese tad-itara sama-dhir yasya va naraki sah.* This is the translation: "Only a person who has a hellish mentality can think that the Deity of Vishnu is a statue, that the Guru is an ordinary human being, that a Vaishnava can be judged based on his birth, that Vishnu and the Vaishnavas can be touched by the contamination of the Kali yuga, that a sacred place of pilgrimage is just a water reservoir, that the mantra constituted by the name of Vishnu is just an ordinary sound, or that the Supreme Lord, Vishnu, is an ordinary person."

In the *Padma purana* Lomasa Rishi declares, *sudram va bhagavad bhaktam nisadam svapacam tatha viksatam jati samanyat sa yati narakam dhruvam*, "A devotee of the Lord may have taken birth in a family of *sudras, nishadas* or *sva-pachas*, but those who evaluate him on the basis of his birth are destined to fall into a hellish condition." In the same text, Vishnu himself states, *na me bhaktas caturvedi mad-bhaktah svapachah priyah, tasmai deyam tato grahyam sa ca pujyo yatha hy aham*, "Even if he was born as a *sva-pacha*, my devotee is dearer to me than one who is expert in reciting the four *Vedas*. His touch is purifying, and he is as worshipable as me."

The *Padma Purana* states, *na sudra bhagavad-bhaktas te tu bhagavata matah sarva-varnesu te sudra ye na bhakta janardane*, "A devotee of God should never be considered a *sudra*, while those who are devoid of devotion must be considered *sudras*, irrespective of the *varna* of the family where they were born." And again, *sva-pacham iva nekseta loke vipram avaisnavam vaisnavo varno-bahyo 'pi punati bhuvana-trayam*, "If a person born as a *brahmana* is devoid of devotion to Vishnu, he should be avoided just like we avoid the contact with a *sva-pacha*. On the other hand, a devotee of Vishnu has the power to purify the three worlds, even if he was born outside the social system of the *varnas*."

It is important to understand that being "a devotee of Vishnu" is not just about some external demonstration of superficial or fanatical devotion to a particular form of the Deity, but it must be sustained in practice by the level of consciousness and behavior that is characteristic of pure *sattva*.

One of the most famous examples is the famous Rishi Satyakama Jabala, whose story is told in the *Chandogya Upanisad* (4.4.1-5): "Satyakama, the son of Jabala, told his mother, 'I wish to go to study as a *brahmachari* in the house of the Guru. To which *gotra* (ancestry) do I belong?' Jabala replied, 'My dear child, I do not know who your father is, because during my younger years I worked in many places, and in that period I had you. Simply tell the teacher that your name is Satyakama Jabala.' Thus Satyakama went to Haridrumata Gautama and said, 'I wish to live with you as a *brahmachari*.' Gautama said, 'To which lineage do you belong?' Satyakama simply repeated what his mother told him, and Gautama said, 'Dear boy, only a *brahmana* could be this truthful, therefore you certainly are a *brahmana* and I accept you as such. Go now to get the firewood to kindle the sacred fire. And never abandon truthfulness."

In his commentary to the *Chandogya Upanishad*, Madhvacharya writes, *arjavam brahmane saksat sudro'narjava- laksanah, gautamas tviti vijnaya satyakamam upanayat*, "A *brahmana* is recognized by the quality of simplicity, while a *sudra* is recognized by his contorted mentality. Knowing this fact, Gautama accepted Satyakama as a disciple."

As we have already mentioned, Veda Vyasa and Valmiki are other famous persons who became known as full fledged *brahmanas* in spite of their birth in families of low condition. Vyasa had a *brahmana* son (Sukadeva), two *kshatriya* sons (Pandu and Dhritarastra) and a son that was situated on a level of consciousness that was completely transcendental to the *varna* system (Vidura).

Visvamitra son of Maharaja Gadi and Maharaja Vitahavya became *brahmanas* although they were born in *kshatriya* families; they are mentioned precisely in this regard in *Mahabharata* respectively in Adi Parva chapter 174 and Anusasana Parva, chapter 30. The story of Visvamitra, who became the *guru* of Rama and Lakshmana the sons of Dasaratha, is very famous because it is found in *Ramayana* and in several *Puranas* as well. Vitahavya attained the level of *brahmana* due to the blessing of Bhrigu Muni. Also the son of Vitahavya, Gritsamada, became a *brahmana*, and so his descendents Suceta, Prakasa, Pramiti (very expert in *Veda* and *Vedanga*), Sunaka, and his son Saunaka Rishi (who narrated the *Bhagavata purana* to the Rishis assembled in Naimisharanya). The *Hari vamsa* (29.7-8) also says that among the descendants of Gritsamada there were many *brahmanas*, as well as *kshatriyas, vaisyas* and *sudras*.

Another *kshatriya* who became a *brahmana* and generated a descendence of *brahmanas* was Maharaja Dhrista, mentioned in *Bhagavata purana* (9.2.16-17). Again the *Bhagavata purana* (9.2.22) mentions for the same reason Maharaja Agnivesya, son of Devadatta, whose *brahmana* descendants became famous as the Agnivesyayanas. We must also remember Jahnu Muni born as the son of king Hotra of the Chandra vamsa (*Bhagavata* 9.15.1-4), Kanva Rishi born in the dynasty of Maharaja Puru and his son Medhatithi who was the ancestor of the *brahmanas* Praskanna (*Bhagavata* 9.20.1-7), Gargya the son of King Sini, the three sons of King Duritakshaya called Trayyaruni, Kavi and Puskararuni (*Bhagavata* 9.21.19); Ajamidha and his son Priyamedha and his descendents such as the great Rishi Mudgala (9.21.21, 9.21.31).

Also, the *Bhagavata* informs us that among the 100 sons of king Rishabhadeva, 81 became *brahmanas* (5.4.13) and that the *vaisyas* Nabhaga and Dista later became *brahmanas* (8.18.3). The *Hari vamsa* (31.33-35) states that Maharaja Bali had 5 *kshatriya* sons but also other sons who were *brahmanas* and generated *brahmana* lineages.

Another important thing is the concept of adopted son or disciple, that according to Vedic culture is perfectly equivalent to the concept of seminal son, both at the social and the legal level, to all effects.

On the other hand, one who was born in a family of *brahmanas* but does not possess the required abilities and tendencies is called *brahma bandhu*, or "relative of *brahmanas*". This is the definition given by *Chandogya Upanishad*: *asmat kulino 'nanucya brahma-bandhur iva bhavati,* "A *brahma bandhu*, a relative of *brahmanas*, is a person who belongs to a family of *brahmanas* but has failed to study the *Vedas*." In his commentary to this verse, Adi Shankaracharya writes, *he saumya ananucya anadhitya brahma-bandhur iva bhavatiti, brahmanan bandhun vyapadisati, na svayam brahmana-vrtah*, "One who has not studied the *Vedas* (in spite of being born from *brahmana* parents) is simply a relative or kinsman of *brahmanas*. He can call such *brahmanas* his dear and near, but he does not have the required behavior to qualify personally as a *brahmana*."

The definitions of *brahma bandhu* ("relative of *brahmanas*) and *brahma atma-ja* ("son of a *brahmana*") is used by Krishna in the *Bhagavata purana* to refer to Asvatthama the son of Drona (1.7.19, 1.7.35) and to describe the general category of unqualified persons (*dvija-bandhu*) for whom Vyasa compiled the *Mahabharata* (1.4.25). *Dvija-bandhu*, or "relative of twice-born" is used not only to describe the unqualified sons of *brahmana* parents, but also for the unqualified children of *kshatriyas* and *vaisyas*, because *kshatriyas* and *vaisyas* too receive the sacred thread in the religious initiation that constitutes the second birth of an *arya*. Sometimes in the Vedic scriptures we find the definition *kshatra bandhu* to refer to some unworthy descendent of *kshatriyas*. The lack of particular qualifications in the sons of *vaisyas* or entrepreneurs is considered less serious, and not dangerous in the administration of society, therefore it is not mentioned.

This applies to the sons of *brahmanas* who, due to their individual nature, are lacking the personal qualifications that are characteristic of the *brahmanas* in regard to *guna* (qualities) and *karma* (activities). So what is, according to the Vedic scriptures, the position of a person who had previously been recognized as *brahmana* but for one reason or another falls to a lower level of consciousness or behavior?

The *Manu samhita* (4.245) states, *uttamanuttaman gacchan hinam hinams ca varjayan, brahmanah sresthatam eti pratyavayena sudratam*, "According to the good or bad company he keeps, a *brahmana* can become extraordinarily elevated or even a *sudra*."

The *Kurma purana* explains: *go-raksakan vanijakan tatha karuka-silinah, presyan vardhusikams caiva vipran sudra-vad acaret, yo'nyatra kurute yatnam, anadhitya srutim dvijah sa sammudho na sambhasyo veda-bahyo dvijatibhih*, "Those *brahmanas* who earn a livelihood by raising cattle, by trade, by artistic shows, by the service to others, or by lending money on interest, are nothing but *sudras*. One who does not study the *Vedas*, but carefully engages in other activities is certainly a foolish person and must be ostracized from the Vedic society - the (true) *brahmanas* should not even talk to him."

It is important to understand that Vedic tradition accepts as valid those improper actions that were performed due to emergency considerations. The *Bhagavata purana* (11.17.47) states that in case of serious financial constraints a *brahmana* can temporarily engage in the occupations that are characteristic of the *vaisyas* or the *kshatriyas*, but he must consider such activities as an emergency action, and return as soon as possible to the activities that are characteristic of the *brahmanas*, otherwise he will lose his social position as a *brahmana* and acquire the position of the activities that he performs continuously.

Particularly serious and degrading is the case of a *brahmana* who chooses to perform the activities that are characteristic of the *sudra*, such as service under salary, even to the government (*raja sevakan*), employed teacher against a salary (*bhrtakadhyapakan*), employee in banking or trade (*vanijakan*), technician of any kind (*yantra-vidyakan*), medical doctor or pharmacist (*cikitisikan*). Even worse are those activities that are based simply on the use of one's body, such as the show business - the performances of dancers, singers, actors, professional reciters, painters, sculptors, craftsmen and so on - as well as personal service to others, especially to persons who are on the level of *sudras* or even worse, of *anaryas*. Such professional occupations are not negative in themselves, but because they are aimed at the satisfaction of the customer and depend on it, they create a situation of dependence and reinforce the identification with the material body: therefore they are completely incompatible with the duties of the *brahmana*.

Neglecting to study and to understand the Vedic scriptures (*svadhyaya tyaga*) still remains the most serious cause for degradation for a son of *brahmana* parents. The *Vishnu dharma shastra* (93.7) states, *yaitral-laksyate sarpa vrttam sa brahmanah smrtah yatraitan na bhavet sarpa tam sudram iti nirdiset, na vary api prayacchet tu vaidala-vratike dvije na baka-vratike vipre naveda vidi dharma-vit*, "Persons who observe the religious teachings should not offer even a drop of water to a hypocrite that, in spite of being the son of a *brahmana*, behaves in a way that is contrary to the laws of ethics."

Manu samhita (2.157, 2.172) states, *yatha kastha-mayo hasti yatha carma-mayo mrgah yas ca vipro'nadhiyanas trayas te nama bibhrati*, "A *brahmana* who does not study the *Vedas* is comparable to an elephant or deer made of leather, that are called elephant or deer but cannot function as such. We must know that as long as a *brahmana* is not qualified in the Vedic knowledge, he remains on the same level of a *sudra*."

Traditionally, a *brahmana* is considered fallen from his social position if he commits violations to purity, for example because of the consumption of non-vegetarian foods, alcoholic drinks, or even of vegetarian foods that have been cooked by *sudras* (*sudranna pustam*), as confirmed by the *Kurma purana*: *nadyac chudrasya vipro'nnam mohad va yadi kamatah sa sudra-yonim vrajati yas tu bhunkte hy-anapadi*. This is the reason why a *brahmana* never goes to a restaurant for eating, and is extremely careful about what he purchases on the market.

The *Mahabharata* (Santi parva, 189.7) declares, *himsanrta-priya lubdhah sarva-karmopjivinah krsna saucaparibhrasthast e dvijah sudratam gatah sarva-bhaksyaratirn ityam sarva-karmakaro 'sucih tyakta-vedastvanaca rah sa vai sudra iti smrtah*, "A *brahmana* who commits violent acts (as for example in the consumption of non-vegetarian foods), who lies and cheats, who is greedy, impure, or engages in any activity in order to earn a livelihood, is degraded to the position of *sudra*. Precisely because he eats and drinks anything without discrimination and is attached to the material things and to the idea of making money, he has abandoned Vedic dharma and ethical behavior, and is called a *sudra*."

It is said that because of the negative influences of the age in which we live, the Kali yuga ("the black age") we should expect an increasing degradation for all the social categories. The *Padma purana* states, *brahmanah ksatriya vaisah sudrah papa-parayanah nijacara-vihinas ca bhavisyanti kalau yuge, vipra veda-vihinas ca pratigraha-parayana hatyanta-kaminah krur bhavisyanti kalau yuge, veda-nindakaras caiva dyutacaurya karas tatha, vidhva-sanga- lubdhas ca bhavisyanti kalau dvijah, vrttyartham brahmanah kecit mahakapata-dharminah, raktambara bhavisyanti jatilah smasrudharinah, kalau yuge bhavisyanti brahmanah sudra-dharmina.* This is translation: "In Kali yuga, all the four social categories become degraded, abandoning the proper behavior, and fall into activities that are contrary to ethics. The *brahmanas* do not study Vedic knowledge and do not perform sacrifices, and abandoning the five ritual duties prescribed in the Vedas and the level of spiritual consciousness, they engage in other activities, even while still claiming the social position (of *brahmanas*) in order to collect money and ask for donations, that they will utilize to satisfy their unlimited desires for sense gratification. The so-called *brahmanas* of Kali yuga are afflicted by lust and cruelty, malice and envy, and become professional thieves, blaspheming the Vedic scriptures, getting drunk and exploiting women for sexual pleasure. They even come to the point of wearing the red robes of the *sadhus*, growing long beard and hair, in order to better cheat the people."

Many examples of degraded *brahmanas* can be found in the scriptures as well as in the more recent historical tradition - from the young Sringhi, the son of Samika Rishi, who cursed Maharaja Parikshit to die within 7 days to avenge himself of a silly joke, to the entire generations of corrupt priests whose nefarious activities in the distortion of the Vedic ritual sacrifices prepared the way to the Buddhist revolution and to the decadence of Indian society.

Even among the followers of Buddhism and Jainism we find many *brahmanas* who openly rejected the authority of Vedic scriptures rather than condemning its distortion - for example Boddhidharma, Buddhapalita, Nagarjuna, Asvaghosa, Asanga, Kumarajiva, Dinnaga, Dharmakirti, Chandrakirti, Santideva and Ratnakirti for Buddhism, and Prabhachandra, Anantavirya, Devasuri, Hemacandra, Nemichandra, Mallisena, and Siddhasena Divakara for Jainism. What to speak of the innumerable *brahmanas* who chose to convert to Islam during the muslim invasions and domination, or the many *brahmanas* who, out of greed or foolishness, cooperated with the British colonialists to the distortion of the Vedic scriptures and to the translation of the Christian propaganda into the Indian languages.

The *Varaha purana* even states, *raksasah kalim asritya jayante brahma-yonisu utpanna brahmana-kule badhante srotriyan krsan*, "Some who were demoniac beings in their previous lifetimes will be born in Kali yuga in *brahmana* families with the purpose of weakening and destroying the tradition of *sruti* (of Vedic scriptures)."

Obviously this situation was exploited as much as possible by the colonialists, as we have already mentioned in our first chapter. Only recently Hindu society is trying to become free from the shackles of the colonial mentality and to rediscover the genuine version of the Vedic scriptures. For example Dr. Raj Pandit Sharma, member of the managing committee of the Hindu Council of the United Kingdom has prepared an important report on this topic - which has been published by his organization and approved by the Shiri Guru Valmik Sabha of Southall in Londra, the official organization of the so-called hindu outcaste. The report states: "It was the British who single-handedly formulated the caste schedules that remain in place today. The evils manifest in the current form of the caste system can not be ascribed to the Hindu faith. The current adulteration of the Hindu *varnashrama* system is a direct result of generations of British Colonial bureaucracy."

Already Swami Vivekananda wrote: "The plan in India is to make everybody Brahmana, the Brahmana being the ideal of humanity. If you read the history of India you will find that attempts have always been made to raise the lower classes. Many are the classes that have been raised. Many more will follow till the whole will become Brahmana. That is the plan. Our ideal is the Brahmana of spiritual culture and renunciation. By the Brahmana ideal what do I mean? I mean the ideal Brahmana-ness in which worldliness is altogether absent and true wisdom is abundantly present.

We read in the Mahabharata that the whole world was in the beginning peopled with Brahmanas, and that as they began to degenerate they became divided into different castes, and that when the cycle turns round they will all go back to that Brahmanical origin. The son of a Brahmana is not necessarily always a Brahmana; though there is every possibility of his being one, he may not become so.

As there are *sattva, rajas* and *tamas* - one or other of these *gunas* more or less - in every man, so the qualities which make a Brahmana, Kshatriya, Vaishya or a Shudra are inherent in every man, more or less. But at time one or other of these qualities predominates in him in varying degrees and is manifested accordingly. Take a man in his different pursuits, for example: when he is engaged in serving another for pay, he is in Shudra-hood; when he is busy transacting some piece of business for profit, on his account, he is a Vaishya; when he fights to right wrongs then the qualities of a Kshatriya come out in him; and when he meditates on God, or passes his time in conversation about Him, then he is a Brahmana. Naturally, it is quite possible for one to be changed from one caste into another. Otherwise, how did Viswamitra become a Brahmana and Parashurama a Kshatriya?

Formerly the characteristic of the noble-minded was (*tri bhuvanam upakara shrenibhih priyamanah*) 'to please the whole universe by one's numerous acts of service', but now it is - I am pure and the whole world is impure. 'Don't touch me!' 'Don't touch me!' The whole world is impure, and I alone am pure! Lucid Brahma-jnana! Bravo! Great God! Nowadays, Brahman is neither in the recesses of the heart, nor in the highest heaven, nor in all beings - now He is in the cooking pot! We are orthodox Hindus, but we refuse entirely to identify ourselves with 'Don't touchism'. That is not Hinduism; it is in none of our books; it is an orthodox superstition, which has interfered with national efficiency all along the line. Religion has entered in the cooking pot. The present religion of the Hindus is neither the path of Knowledge or Reason - it is 'Don't-touchism'. - 'Don't touch me', 'Don't touch me' - that exhausts its description. 'Don't touchism' is a form of mental disease. See that you do not lose your lives in this dire irreligion of 'Don't- touchism'.

Must the teaching (*Atmavat sarva bhuteshu*) - 'Looking upon all beings as your own self' - be confined to books alone? How will they grant salvation who cannot feed a hungry mouth with a crumb of bread? How will those, who become impure at the mere breath of others, purify others?

I sometimes feel the urge to break the barriers of 'Don't-touchism', go at once and call out, 'Come all who are poor, miserable, wretched and downtrodden', and to bring them all together. Unless they rise, the Mother will not awake. Each Hindu, I say, is a brother to every other, and it is we, who have degraded them by our outcry, 'Don't touch', 'Don't touch!' And so the whole country has been plunged to the utmost depths of meanness, cowardice and ignorance.

Our solution of the caste question is not degrading those who are already high up, is not running amock through food and drink, is not jumping out of our own limits in order to have more enjoyment, but it comes by every one of us fulfilling the dictates of our Vedantic religion, by our attaining spirituality and by our becoming ideal Brahmana.

The command is the same to you all, that you must make progress without stopping, and that from the highest man to the lowest pariah, every one in this country has to try and become the ideal Brahmana.

This Vedantic idea is applicable not only here but over the whole world. The Brahmana-hood is the ideal of humanity in India as wonderfully put forward by Shankaracharya at the beginning of his commentary on the Gita, where he speaks about the reason for Krishna's coming as a preacher for the preservation of Brahmana- hood, of Brahmana-ness. That was the great end. This Brahmana, the man of God, he who has known Brahman, the ideal man, the perfect man, must remain, he must not go. And with all the defects of the caste now, we know that we must all be ready to give to the Brahmanas this credit, that from them have come more men with real Brahmana-ness in them than from all the other castes. We must be bold enough, must be brave enough to speak their defects, but at the same time we must give credit that is due to them. Therefore, it is no use fighting among the castes. What good will it do? It will divide us all the more, weaken us all the more, degrade us all the more. It seems that most of the Brahmanas are only nursing a false pride of birth; and any schemer, native or foreign, who can pander to this vanity and inherent laziness, by fulsome sophistry, appears to satisfy more."

Vivekananda's diagnosis is precise. Those who were born in "traditionally qualified" families but do not make the effort required to qualify personally through the study of the scriptures and proper behavior, life style and spiritual practices, end up by creating an atmosphere of cynicism, more or less unconscious inferiority/ superiority complexes, fear, sense of dissatisfaction, that are covered and hidden by arrogance and aggressiveness. When such imbalanced persons insist in claiming that the study of Vedic scriptures is their exclusive birth right, and cannot be legitimately taken up by persons who were born in family of a different origin, they enforce on society in general the impression that trying to become spiritually qualified is a useless pursuit, at least in this lifetime.

Because the degrading tendencies of Kali yuga are dragging down all those who fail to sincerely make efforts to progress and elevate themselves, even those who have some good tendencies and a good potential for development end up falling back into laziness and indifference, thus wasting the valuable opportunity of human birth.

This situation did not happen by chance. The accusation of the Hindu Council is well founded.

As we have seen in the previous chapter, the British colonial government was certainly interested in weakening the Vedic ideology, so that the Indian subcontinent could more easily be dominated. And certainly there was some malice in their introducing the notorious Aryan Invasion Theory and the idea of the caucasian origin of the so-called indo-european race. The idea that the Vedic culture had been introduced to India by the so-called indo-european aryans, of white race, was presented as the justification rationale of the superiority of the "white" civilization on racial basis. To understand the origin of this theory and its fallacy, we need to clarify some important Vedic concepts, defined as *varna, kula, gotra, vamsa* and *jati*. We have already seen that *varna* is the social position, including rights and duties, of the four professional categories defined as *brahmanas, kshatriyas, vaisyas* and *sudras* - respectively intellectuals, administrators, entrepreneurs and laborers.

The word *kula* refers to the "family" or "house" to which one belongs - by birth or by choice - in a permanent or temporary way. For example, the house of the Guru where the students live during their *brahmacharya* period is called Guru Kula. This word also applies to religious associations, especially in the tantric field, where the initiated members consider themselves as belonging to the same family.

The words *gotra* and *vamsa* indicate seminal descent, or the origin of a particular family descending from a founder of the "dynasty", respectively for *brahmanas* (*gotra*) and *kshatriyas* (*vamsa*). The descendents of *brahmanas* and *kshatriyas* are (or should be) aware of the responsibilities that derive from their family heritage, and make all the necessary efforts to cultivate the qualities (*guna*) and activities (*karma*) that make them worthy of their ancestors and constitute a brilliant example for the personal development for their own children. This is about a relationship of affection, gratitude and respect, of a veritable debt (*rina*) that must be repaid, both by ritually honoring the memory of one's ancestors and by adequately training one's descendants. As in the case of the *varna*, membership in the *gotra* can also be modified in the course of one's lifetime, especially with the ostracism of an unworthy descendent.

A different situation concerns *jati* or "birth", that exclusively relates to the genetic condition, that enables (or not) the individual to physically perform particular duties through fundamental characteristics and abilities of the body and the mind. Vedic scriptures describe 3 types of *jati*: *manusya jati* ("birth as a human being"), *pakshi jati* ("birth as a bird") and *mriga jati* ("birth as a mammal animal").

The British propagandists erroneously grafted the concept of *jati* on their own pseudo-scientific ideas on racial anthropology that had been brewing in Europe from the times of Carl Linnaeus (1707-1778), the famous physician, botanist, and zoologist. In *Systema Naturae* (1767) he wrote of five human races: the white *Europeanus* of gentle character and inventive mind, the red *Americanus* of stubborn character and angered easily; the the black *Africanus* relaxed and negligent; yellow *Asiaticus* avaricious and easily distracted; and the *Monstrosus* sub humans such as aborigines. Even thinkers such as Friedrich Hegel, Immanuel Kant and

Auguste Comte believed that western European culture was the acme of human socio-cultural evolution in a linear process, and approved slavery of "inferior races". In their *Indigenous Races of the Earth Before Origin of Species* (1850), Josiah Clark Nott and George Robins Gliddon implied that "negroes" were a creational rank between "Greeks" (considered the beginning of western European culture) and chimpanzees.

Non-white people were kept in cages at "human zoos" during colonial exhibitions promoting the benefits of white colonialism to such colored peoples. In 1906 a Pygmy named Ota Benga was displayed as the "Missing Link", in the Bronx Zoo, New York City, alongside apes and animals. Several others examples are recorded.

Max Müller is often identified as the first writer to speak of an Aryan "race". In 1861 in his *Lectures on the Science of Language* he referred to Aryans as a "race of people". Müller was responding to the development of racial anthropology and to the influence of the work of Arthur de Gobineau who argued that the Indo-Europeans represented a superior branch of humanity.

A number of later writers, such as the French anthropologist Vacher de Lapouge in his book *L'Aryen* argued that this superior branch could be identified biologically by using the cephalic index (a measure of head shape) and other indicators. He argued that the long-headed "dolichocephalic-blond" Europeans, characteristically found in northern Europe, were natural leaders, destined to rule over more "brachiocephalic" (short headed) peoples.

In the 18th century an early physical anthropologist, the American physician Samuel George Morton (1799-1851), collected human skulls from around the world and attempted a logical classification scheme. Influenced by the contemporary racialist theory, Dr Morton said he could judge racial intellectual capacity by measuring the interior cranial capacity - ergo a large skull denoted a large brain, thus high intellectual capacity; conversely, a small skull denoted a small brain, thus low intellectual capacity. Of course nobody noticed that the cranial capacity of Neanderthals was much larger compared to the Cro Magnons', the modern type of man that is the supposed result of progressive evolution - or that in proportion to the total weight of the body, a rat's brain constitutes the maximum brain capacity of all species, including the human species.

In the United States, scientific racism justified Black African slavery to curb the moral opposition to the Atlantic slave trade. Alexander Thomas and Samuell Sillen described black men as uniquely fitted for bondage because of their "primitive psychological organization". In 1851, in antebellum Louisiana, the physician Samuel A. Cartwright (1793–1863) labeled the escape attempts of slaves as "drapetomania", a kind of mental illness, and wrote that "with proper medical advice, strictly followed, this troublesome practice that many Negroes have of running away can be almost entirely prevented". After the Civil War, Southern

(Confederacy) physicians wrote textbooks of scientific racism based upon studies claiming that black freemen (ex-slaves) were becoming extinct because they were inadequate to the demands of being a free man, implying that black people actually benefited from enslavement.

With the purpose of gaining support from the "highest breeds" of India, British ideologists formulated the "Aryan invasion theory", according to which some foreign invaders, the white "Aryan" nomadic or semi-nomadic tribes coming from Central Northern Asia (i.e. Caucasus, hence "Caucasian race") had swept into India around 1500 BCE and conquered the primitive and pacific civilization of black Dravidians by means of superior iron weaponry, chariots and horses. According to this theory, the stronger, war-mongering and ruthless invaders killed the "primitive indigenous tribes" by the thousands, enslaved some of them and drove the rest away to South India.

Thus India was supposedly "civilized" by these typically white nomads with the introduction of Vedic knowledge and Sanskrit, and the division of social classes where the two higher and dominating classes (*brahmanas* and *kshatriyas*) were of "pure Aryan race", the third class (the *vaisyas*) was a mixture of the conquerors and the conquered, and the fourth and lowest class (*sudra*) was composed by the enslaved conquered "primitive and racially inferior" (black) Dravidians. The same theory also affirmed that Aryan peoples invaded Europe, too, where they became the dominant race, identified by

Nazi theories as stout and tall white people with blond hair and blue eyes.

The above described "Aryan invasion theory" has been amply discredited by many archaeological finds, starting from 1922 with the discovery of the remains of Mohenjo Daro and Harappa, two highly developed and civilized urban settlements that have been dated much earlier than 1500 BCE. The most ancient of such urban settlements, Mehrgarh, is presently dated around 7000 BCE, while the largest - Lakhmirwala and Rakhigarhi - covered 225 hectares each, more than double the area of Mohenjo Daro and Harappa.

While it is perfectly possible that around 1500 BCE a wave of barbaric and nomadic invaders actually came down into India from the Caucasus, as this also happened several centuries later with the Huns and other similar populations, the result of such marginal invasions could not be the introduction of Sanskrit and Vedic knowledge with a "civilizing effect". As such, these barbaric and nomadic invaders could not possibly have been a "superior race of civilizers".

Why? Simply because the *aryas*, i.e. the people following Vedic civilization, Sanskrit and the Vedas were already in India, with a presence that dates back several thousands years. In all the Vedic scriptures or in the oral tradition there is absolutely no mention of a previous place of origin of the *aryas* that was not the Indian subcontinent, from which the *aryas* might have "migrated".

The revolutionary discovery of Mohenjo Daro and Harappa was the mind-boggling testimony of a highly refined urban civilization, with modern sanitary works (each house had a bathroom connected to a city sewage system running under the paved streets, with regular manholes for inspection), shopping complexes, public granaries, swimming pools, and rounded corners in the ample streets to ease the passage and turning of large vehicles. People used to wear cotton clothes, decorated themselves with complex ornaments and hair arrangements, used containers made of vitrous ceramic and had developed a flourishing river-born commercial trade. The houses had worship rooms (centered around the Vedic system of fire sacrifice, as well as images of Shiva, Durga, and other vedic Deities) and among the great wealth of seals discovered, many seals depict Vedic deities, the bull, and other classical Vedic symbols.

Today we know of more than 1,000 similar sites with remains of urbanized settlements along the valleys of ancient Sindhu and Sarasvati, spread across a territory that includes present Pakistan and Afghanistan besides India. The ancient Sarasvati river is particularly interesting as it dried up more than 5000 years ago, yet it is amply described in Vedic texts as a very important and large river. Western scholars used to consider the river Sarasvati a mere legend or a symbolic figure, until its huge dry bed was located by satellite photos. The drying of the Sarasvati river, that occurred around the same period of the drying of the Sahara region in Africa, seems to be the most likely reason why these areas were abandoned, when their inhabitants went to join the other very ancient cities of the Ganga plains, such as - for example - Prayaga (presently known as Allahabad) and Kasi (also known as Varanasi or Benares).

The long academic success of the Aryan Invasion Theory (still taught in schools in India and at global level as an historically proven and unquestionable fact) is even more disconcerting when we take the pain of actually reading the *Vedas* and Vedic literature, and find that they always describe a highly urbanized, prosperous, settled and refined Vedic society which does not tally with the inevitably limited conditions of nomadic life or even with the desolate, arid and mountainous territory of Caucasus which was supposed to be the "place of origin" of the so-called Aryan race.

People that are constantly on the move as a way of life do not build cities, palaces, or temples. Rather, they need to live very simply in tents, preferably made of animal skins (as hunting is an important resource of nomads) that can be packed and moved easily, as we can see still today in the populations that continue to live in this way.

Nomads are people who are constantly on the move as a life style, therefore they never build cities, palaces or temples: they are forced to keep the material possessions to a minimum that can be transported easily (which usually do not include books) and do not have complex knowledge. The nomads' culture is transmitted orally, around the camp fires, and religion is usually of a shamanic type. Even simple craftsmanship is reduced to the minimum because there is a tendency to abandon those utensils that are not strictly necessary and to build new ones when the next camp is set.

In nomadic life cattle herding is only practical when the animals are regularly slaughtered for meat, especially the young and old ones that cannot move quickly with the tribe when it's time to move the camp. On the contrary, we see that Vedic civilization never contemplates the slaughtering of cattle (especially calves), rather considering it a very heinous sin. Even separating the calf from the mother is considered an act contrary to religiosity. A nomadic life is naturally dependent on hunting and pillaging rather than agriculture (that requires a settled life) and marginally with the occasional gathering of spontaneously growing vegetables.

All the accounts of Vedic civilization, in the form of the many stories they contain astronomical references even dating back to hundreds of thousands of years, show a great development of settled agriculture based on cultivation of cereals, a preference towards ethical vegetarianism, non-violence and peacefulness, and a system of social classes based on the natural tendencies of each single individual, no matter what color or race. The Aryans they describe were not a genetically superior race but a civilized society to which anyone could be admitted.

Similarly, the chronology accepted by mainstream academic institutions and textbooks for the compilation of the Vedic scriptures, based on the Aryan Invasion Theory, seems to be highly biased and above all it does not correspond with what the Vedas themselves tell.

Still in the 20th century, the dating of ancient civilizations were influenced by the belief of many scholars and archaeologists, including the famous Max Muller, according to which the creation of the world had been established in 4004 BCE, and the Great Flood described in the Bible in 2500 BCE. Even when the Bible's version was disproved by the discovery of fossils and by the growing popularity of Darwin's evolutionary theory, academy maintained the belief that until a few thousands years before Christ, the entire mankind had been living in an extremely primitive state, slowly evolving from the Stone Age (up to 3000 BCE) to the Iron Age (starting around 600 BCE) with the most ancient civilizations located in Sumer, in the middle east and in Egypt, between 3500 and 2200 BCE, then in Greece and in the Roman Empire, while the rest of the world was more or less immersed in a barbaric state up to the colonial period.

With the end of colonialism and the establishment of the humanistic values and the independent scientific research in the fields of anthropology and archeology, many old myths of indology have justly been exposed. The very perspective on ancient history has been deeply transformed, thanks to many revolutionary discoveries in the last century, that "set back the clock" on the history of human race several thousands years. Unfortunately the outdated model of the history of mankind is still taught in the majority of the school texts, especially those for the primary schools.

Later on, the nazi theories on the aryan race have unjustly burdened the word "aryan" (and the symbol of *svastika*, also stolen from the vedic culture) with a very unhappy association with the negative concepts of racism, oppression and violence, that are expressed in our days with the "politically correct" euphemism *ethnic cleansing*.

The resurgence of Vedic culture in India had to struggle against all these huge difficulties. In the beginning, under the British colonial regime, the only chance of survival consisted in presenting Vedic knowledge in a format that could be acceptable to the victorian British mentality, and this was the origin of the so-called neo-Hinduism or "reformed" Hinduism.

Among the famous teachers that started to spread the spiritual message of Sanatana Dharma in English language still during the British colonial regime in India we remember Ramakrishna (1836-1886) and especially his disciple Vivekananda (1863-1902), Bhaktivinoda (1838-1914) and his son Bhaktisiddhanta (1874-1936), Aurobindo (1872-1950), Ram Tirtha (1873-1906), Ramana Maharshi (1879-1950), Swami Ramdas (1884-1963), Swami Sivananda (1887-1963), Sarvepalli Radhakrishnan (1888-1975), Paramahamsa Yogananda (1893-1952) and Swami Chinmayananda (1916-1993).

This presentation of the Vedic tradition to the western work by Indian preachers started as a reaction to the denigratory comments given by the majority of the officers of the colonial empire and by the European scholars that visited the British colonies. The first stage was some kind of "reform of Hinduism" meant to give a secondary place or to eliminate altogether those ideas that seemed to be most difficult to digest for the sensitivity of the British officers, academics and religious missionaries - specifically, anglican protestants.

The first of these groups, the movement called Brahmo samaj (1820) founded by Ram Mohan Roy (1772-1833), was strongly influenced by the teachings of the Unitarian Church and by the syncretist concept of the Radical Universalism. Roy wrote a treatise entitled *The Precepts of Jesus: The Guide to Peace and Happiness*, and he learned Hebrew and Greek to study the Bible and translate it into Bengali, with the idea of "purifying" and "modernizing" Vedic tradition, by merging it with Christianity, Hebraism, Islam and Buddhism. The ideology of the Brahmo samaj rejected the worship to the sacred images (which they called "graven images" and "idols"), the validity of the sacred stories of *Puranas* and *Itihasas* (which they called mythology), the tradition of the temples and the holy places of pilgrimage (which they called superstition) and the multiplicity of the Personalities of Godhead (which they called demigods). It also rejected the system of *varnas* or social categories, the offerings in the memory of the deceased, and whatever component of the Vedic tradition could appear as "pagan" or somehow unacceptable for the victorian moralism of that period. It only retained those aspects that it considered "respectable", such as the highly symbolic hymns of *Rig, Sama, Yajur* and *Atharva Veda* (translated in a practically incomprehensible way and impossible to apply into some practical or useful knowledge) and the concept of Brahman as God or Universal Spirit or Logos as explained in some *Upanishads*. A similar ideology, albeit less openly servile towards the British missionaries and the other religions, was affirmed by the Prarthana samaj and by the subsequent Arya samaj (1875), still surviving and prospering - and bizarrely considered one of the most authoritative official representatives of traditional hinduism, especially by the government.

Swami Dayananda Sarasvati (1824-1883) founder of the Arya samaj, strongly condemned the "idol worship, ritualism, legends and superstitions" of the Hindu tradition, exalting instead the philosophical speculation on the four original branches of *Rig, Sama, Yajur* and *Atharva Veda* (*Samhitas, Aranyakas* and *Upanishads*), celibacy for the religious students and the meditation on the sacred syllable Om, considered "the real name of God".

He also supported Universalism, or the spreading of knowledge without limitations of nationality or race or religious faith. Briefly joined to the Theosophical Society, the Arya samaj became the inspiration for many other "Hindu reformers" of the colonial period, as well of many western philosophers who were attracted by the eastern ideas in general.

Ramakrishna, who inspired the Ramakrishna Mission founded by his disciple Swami Vivekananda, openly stated he wanted to follow "all religions".

Vivekananda wrote, " I shall go to the Mosque of the Mohammedan; I shall enter the Christian's Church and kneel before the Crucifix; I shall enter the Buddhist Temple, where I shall take refuge in Buddha, and in his Law. I shall go into the forest and sit down in meditation with the Hindu who is trying to see the Light, which enlightens the heart of every one."

Still today the Ramakrishna Mission calls "abbots" its "top monks", compares its "monasteries" to the Essene communities of the times of Jesus Christ and to the Catholic monastic orders, and has openly renounced the Hindu identity by declaring itself "non-hindu organization" in its registration with the Indian government.

It freely celebrates Christmas and Easter, but it does not recognize its western-born disciples as eligible to become authorized gurus to confer initiation in the name of the Math. It also has a separate organization for women, called Sri Sarada Math, because the Ramakrishna Math is strictly for men only.

The ideology of the Ramakrishna Mission states that God is essentially without a form, but he takes personal aspects for the benefit of mankind; however, it discourages the building of temples or altars including private altars in one's own house.

After India obtained independence from the British empire, a slow recovery period started, especially with the help of the second generation of the preachers of Sanatana Dharma - starting from Bhaktivedanta Swami Prabhupada (the famous founder of the Hare Krishna movement), followed by Neem Karoli Baba, Herakhan Babaji, Meher Baba, Mother Meera, Swami Muktananda (Siddha Yoga), Anandamayi, Amritananda Mayi, Osho (Rajneesh), Maharishi Mahesh Yogi, Mataji Nirmala Srivastava (of Sahajya Yoga), Sant Sri Asaramji Bapu (founder of Sri Yog Vedanta Seva Samiti), Sri Sri Ravi Shankar (not the musician, but the head of the Art of Living Foundation) and a growing number of Swamis and Gurus who have accepted millions of disciples among westerners.

The teachings deriving from Vedic knowledge have become extremely popular especially in the form of the various yoga disciplines, with thousands of teachers (Iyengar for example) and natural Ayurvedic medicine with popular names such as Deepak Chopra and many others. Very soon westerners too have moved from the position of disciples to the position of teachers, multiplying the groups, the schools, the centers and the organizations that present such disciplines.

In the last decades western countries have seen a huge increase in the interest for spiritual research through a number of methods of personal growth produced by the New Age culture but inspired by the Indian wisdom - such as rebirthing, the various forms of meditation, creative visualization, conscious dreaming, pranotherapy, spiritual healing and so on.

For a sincere seeker who wants to study the original Vedic knowledge for his/ her own cultural and spiritual progress, free from political, institutional or academic motivations, the best choice is to make the best efforts to go diretly to the source, approaching those who have followed the Vedic knowledge as their own belief system and way of life for innumerable generations on the Indian subcontinent. Although in the course of the centuries Indian culture has being subjected to the superimposition of cultural influences from the Islamic and European domination (especially British), its roots continue to survive almost unchanged by the millennia, in what is today known as traditional Hinduism.

"Hinduism" is a rather controversial definition, because the word *hindu* is never mentioned in the original texts.

Sarvepalli Radhakrishnan wrote: "The Hindu civilization is so called, since it original founders or earliest followers occupied the territory drained by the Sindhu (the Indus) river system corresponding to the North-West Frontier Province and the Punjab... The people on the Indian side of the Sindhu were called Hindu by the Persian and the later western invaders."

Many prefer the Vedic definition of *sanatana dharma*, that can be approximately translated as "the eternal function of the living being", where *sanatana* means "eternal, imperishable". To get a more precise translation of the technical word *sanatana dharma* we need to analyze the deep meanings of the word *dharma*, that contrarily to what many believe, does not exactly correspond to the western idea of "religion". Later on we will elaborate more on this very important concept: now we will simply say that the primary meaning of *dharma* is "the natural law that sustains the universe".

As the eternal and universal law that supports the cosmos, Vedic knowledge is therefore on a level that transcends space and time, and rather exists intrinsically as the "original blueprint" of everything that exists in the universe. From time to time it is perceived, experienced and revealed by the Self realized souls, that transmit it in the form of sacred literature. Thus, it does not have a historic origin in time.

According to tradition, Vedic knowledge was manifested by the creator of the universe, Brahma, at the time of starting to form the various elements of creation. Because it is the natural awareness of reality, the original *Veda* ("knowledge") does not need to be explained or taught, but is directly realized in the heart, in the transcendental awareness of the Self that constitutes the true spiritual nature of all beings, and that is eternity (*sat*), happiness (*ananda*) and knowledge (*cit*). According to Vedic tradition, the individual Self (*atman*) or microcosm is not different from the universal Self (*brahman*) or macrocosm. By realizing his own nature of knowledge, one becomes able to understand the nature of everything, because he obtains the *darshana* of the Reality from which everything emanates.

At the creation of the universe, all human beings were adequately qualified to realize Vedic knowledge in its most complex and concentrated form, orally transmitted in a perfect way thanks to the excellent memory that constitutes the original genetic heritage of human beings. Later on, with the passing of time, the qualities of the human beings became weaker and the original *Veda* had to be explained in a more elaborate way and divided into various categories. Contrarily to the western theory of the progress of mankind, starting from a primitive condition of brute ignorance and culminating with the contemporary technological man (considered the final result of an evolution where survival is obtained thanks to the best characteristics of a species) the Vedic vision speaks of a journey of reverted evolution, or involution, where man's genetic patrimony gradually decays to a minimal part of the original qualities. Then the genetic assets of mankind are renewed cyclically according a calendar of four universal seasons or ages (*yuga*), called respectively Satya, Treta, Dvapara and Kali.

At each cycle of creation of each single universe there is a set of 1000 cycles of four ages constituting one "day" of Brahma, the creator of that particular universe. Each night Brahma withdraws the greatest part of his creation and "puts the rest to sleep" until the next morning. There is also a longer cycle that covers the entire life of Brahma the creator, constituted by 100 of his years, each composed of 365 of his days. Thus it is calculated that in each lifetime of Brahma there are 36.5 million complete cycles of the four ages (365x100x1000). In each of these cycles mankind is created according to the original and perfect genetic project, and the same applies to all the other living species - according to the Vedas there are 4 million 300 thousand species of life, of which 400 thousand are human or humanoid. Not all these species are simultaneously present, because their particular characteristics make them suitable to different circumstances of time and place. This mechanism of incompleteness in the diversity of the species in a particular historical moment can give the impression of an evolution of the darwinian type, but according to the Vedic tradition these are rather cyclic manifestations that may sometimes superimpose, with the continued existence of elementary forms of life (i.e. unevolved bodies) that according to the darwinian theory should have been extinct already. According to the people's ability to understand and work in each period, Vedic knowledge is expressed in more or less extended and complex way. Furthermore, it is said that the extension and the complexity of the Vedic texts are different on the various planets inhabited by the 400 thousand human and humanoid species existing in the universe. The present version of Vedic scriptures existing on this planet and in this particular period (that started about 5 thousand years ago) is the simplest and shortest, because in the age of Kali, in which we live, the potential of the human beings falls to a minimum. It is said that at the beginning of the Kali yuga the *avatara* Vyasa decided to write down this particular compilation precisely to cater to the different needs of the people.

As we have already mentioned, in Satya yuga (the first age of the four), human beings are all qualified to the maximum level - healthy and sound of body and mind, endowed with great intelligence, extraordinary longevity and good fortune, and naturally able to understand and follow the universal principles of *dharma* - austerity, cleanliness, compassion and truthfulness. There were no particular social categories because everybody was able to understand, directly and personally, the subtleties of Vedic knowledge simply by listening to the natural voice of conscience and intuition, without the intervention of teachers or guides. There were no dangers, criminality or wars, and therefore there was no need of warriors or kinds, or of any form of government. As the land spontaneously produced nutritious plants and the cows had a natural production of excess milk, people had plenty of food and other commodities without any need to work in agriculture, trade, or enterprises of any kind. And because everybody was perfectly able to take care of themselves, there was no need for servants or assistants. Therefore the entire population was constituted by *brahmanas*, without any need of *kshatriyas, vaisyas* or *sudras* (what to speak of *chandalas*). For everybody, the method for spiritual and religious realization was the practice of Yoga and meditation on Transcendence, that purifies intelligence from all material identifications and attachments. Renunciation, balance, dutifulness and self-discipline enabled everyone to control the mind and the senses and to engage in the contemplation of the Divine within their own hearts. This ancient happy period saw the rise of Yoga, Sankhya and Tantra, and the expression of the highly symbolic hymns of the original *Veda*.

In the subsequent *yuga* mankind started to become degraded because of the restlessness of the mind and because of strong desires. At first austerity was lost, because people developed a lust for the pleasures of the heavenly planets and the material advantages that can be obtained on this planet: a favorable birth, good descendents, a good wife or husband, fame, wealth and opulence, material power, beauty, physical strength, mental strength, knowledge and so on.

Thus in Treta yuga the *yuga dharma* consists in the ritual performance of sacrifices, in the faithful celebration of the *nitya karmani*, the daily duties that include the *homa* or fire sacrifice. The main qualification, the prime concern for this type of religious practice is cleanliness (*sauca*), therefore tradition gives a huge importance to purification and cleanliness at every step: both externally and internally. Without the proper cleanliness and purity, a person does not have the *adhikara* (right) to perform the traditional rituals, while on the other side as we have seen anyone can become qualified through the proper system of purification and cleanliness.

In the cycle of the universal seasons, Treta yuga is followed by the Dvapara yuga, with a proportional decrease of the qualities of the human beings. Cleanliness becomes difficult to maintain, both internally and externally, therefore the emphasis of religious activities moves towards the more compassionate *yuga dharma* consisting in Deity worship. Although cleanliness and austerity are still recommended, the worship of the Deities in the temple is made accessible to those who do not possess great qualifications in that field, because the mass of people can always assist to the rituals, offer their homage and receive the *prasadam* without having to demonstrate to have any personal qualification. The direct worship of the Deities on the altar is delegated to the *pujakas* that are able to maintain high levels of cleanliness and austerity because they are not required to perform any other work, and they act as intermediaries in the relationship between people in general and the *vigrahas* installed in the temple. Therefore in Dvapara yuga wealthy *kshatriyas* and *vaisyas* take up the responsibility to establish temples and provide to the regular maintenance of the *brahmanas* who perform the rituals in the name of the *karta* (the person that finances the worship and is thus considered its author) and of society and large.

Of course cleanliness is always encouraged, especially for the officiating priests but also for the general visitors, albeit in a lesser degree. For example, the traditional temples always have at least a sacred pool, called *kunda* or *sarovara*, where the devotees or pilgrims can take bath or at least purify themselves a little before entering the temple. However, the main activity of the temple is the compassionate distribution of sanctified food (*prasadam*) and other consecrated offerings such as water, flowers etc, and the performance of lectures and public discussions on the *shastra*, so that the mass of people can obtain the benefit of transcendental knowledge without having to strictly observe the rules of cleanliness or austerity.

The age where we live at present, started about 5 thousand years ago, is the age of Kali, a period of degradation where human decadence reaches a maximum - and then there is a crisis at global level, by which the population of the planet is purified and small groups of persons evolved as qualified *brahmanas* inaugurate a new golden age or Satya yuga, returning to the original version of Vedic knowledge.

Printed in Great Britain
by Amazon